DECOYS

The Art of the Wooden Bird

Richard LeMaster

Contemporary Books, Inc.
Chicago

Library of Congress Cataloging in Publication Data

LeMaster, Richard, 1928–
  Decoys: the art of the wooden bird.

  Includes index.
  1. Decoys (Hunting) I. Title.
SK335.L4   1982   745.593   82-45409
ISBN 0-8092-5664-9

Published by Contemporary Books, Inc.
180 North Michigan Avenue, Chicago, Illinois 60601
Manufactured in the United States of America
Library of Congress Catalog Card Number: 82-45409
International Standard Book Number: 0-8092-5664-9

Published simultaneously in Canada by
Beaverbooks, Ltd.
150 Lesmill Road
Don Mills, Ontario M3B 2T5
Canada

Contents

This book is dedicated to true artists—the decoy makers of the past, present, and future.

Introduction

Decoy making is an original North American folk art that dates back many centuries. From those woven of reeds by Indians to the contemporary wooden sculptures, decoys have a charm all to themselves.

Has the art of decoy making survived because people fancy replicas of waterfowl? Or is it the effectiveness of decoys as used by hunters in the field? Undoubtedly, the tales of their use passed down through generations has played a part in sustaining the art. How decoys sat in the water, how durable they were, how lightweight they were, how well the paint lasted—all of these details about the storyteller's favorite decoys were passed on (and probably embellished) until they became legends. In the field, decoys were rated on how well they lured the quarry close enough for the hunter to shoot it. How the decoy acted in the water was also of prime importance, for if it was not right, the wild ducks might avoid approaching it. In addition, decoys had to be designed to right themselves if overturned by pounding waves. These tales of hunting usually included some mention of "puttin' out the blocks" or how the ducks "swung over the blocks." Time and time again the hunts were relived around a potbellied stove or campfire. Is this the lore that helped turn the wooden decoy into an art form?

Without the success of the decoys' original use, they would have inevitably disappeared. And without the makers' determination to improve the decoys' allure and to produce them in sufficient numbers to meet demand, they would have died out. Another threat to their future as works of art might have come when factories started turning them out in mass quantities. But even these store-bought, wooden decoys did little damage to the appeal of these sculptures.

When plastic decoys were introduced, one would have expected the wooden blocks to lose out entirely. The plastic models were lighter, cheaper, more abundant, and more durable. Who would ever want to hunt with a wooden decoy again? A few purists did—and still do—but the majority switched to plastics as fast as they could afford them. Consequently, many thousands of wooden decoys were used to stoke the potbellied stoves where the tales of the hunt concerned the effectiveness of plastic decoys. The wooden models lost out in field use to plastic decoys because something came along that fit the hunters' needs a little better.

But wooden decoys continued to be made. Evidently their survival through time was not because of their resemblance to waterfowl, nor was it a result of their effectiveness in luring. Wooden decoys will always exist because of their simple beauty of color and form. The emergence of the plastic hunting decoy released the wooden decoy to fulfill the role it had been destined for—an artistic sculpture in wood.

Decoys as Art

The very first time someone set a wooden decoy on the mantel for decoration, the decoy's role as an art form was ensured and affirmed. One did not have to be a hunter—one probably didn't even need to know what kind of duck it represented. The one thing that first admirer did know was that the decoy was pretty. Nonhunters have appreciated the beauty of the wooden decoy every bit as much as, and probably even more than, those who actually used them in the field. The recognition of the decoy as something other than a hunting accessory—as a decorative object—unquestionably confirmed it as an art form. The wooden decoy will retain its place in history as a graceful sculpture.

Thousands of people collect wooden decoys today. Some collect only the antique decoys and some the contemporary works (which will be antiques in time), with the majority of collectors bridging the gap and collecting both.

While in New York on a speaking engagement several years ago, I was challenged by an editor of one of the environmentalist magazines. He gruffly exclaimed that there was more beauty in one of the Ward brothers' decoys than all of my new carvings put together. He really thought that he could shake me up with his statement but I had nothing to disagree with. Beauty is in the eyes of the beholder. I love the Ward brothers' decoys—wish I had a bushel basket of them. Besides, Lem Ward is a friend of mine and I try to visit with him whenever I am in Maryland. To be truthful, I really like *all* of the early decoy makers' works. I enjoy the beauty of the wooden decoys, from antiques to the realistic, contemporary models. Regardless of maker or style, these sculptures are true works of art.

A wooden decoy conveys a feeling that its maker had or has toward waterfowl. Each and every decoy artist has a style all his own. Sometimes they try to copy each other and for a time they may come close, but ultimately their own style will show through. This interchange of styles was a big plus for the early decoy makers. It allowed a lot of latitude in style, though the decoys that rose above the rest often had some design in common. As the decoy movement grew, so did the study of the live duck (or, perhaps, it was the other way around!). New cameras, films, and equipment enabled photographers to capture the subtleties of waterfowl anatomy. When knowledge of anatomy expanded, however, the artistic style seemed to narrow. Many decoy artists turned toward what the duck actually looked like, deemphasizing their artistic feel for the duck's structure. The closer artists come to the real thing, the more uniform the carvings will become. Unless a person has had experience in observing live ducks and their individual traits, even ducks of the same species look alike.

A friend of mine, who is a super carver, insists that this resemblance among other artists' carvings is due to the use of machines for carving and of burning tools for the texture. This may indeed be a contributing factor, however, the more decoys look like a live duck, the more similar they will appear to each other. Of course, little personal touches will always show in an artist's work, but will they be enough to make that soughtafter distinction that becomes the artists' invaluable trademark?

The world of the decoy has seen tremendous growth over the last decade. The old-timers left us a legacy of simple design. On the other hand, the modern trend is the ultimate look-alike of the live duck. There is room for both in the realm of decoys. In time, decoys may eventually be broken into styles, just as styles in painting and sculpture have been distinguished. It would be imprudent to label them as yet, except in the most basic manner. All decoy styles will be accepted— some more than others, perhaps—but the same is true for all forms of art. I do not believe we should all strive for realism, nor do I think stylizing should be the only answer. The ultimate solution lies in the personal touch of each decoy artist.

A Step-by-Step Approach

When I wrote *Wildlife in Wood* (Contemporary Books, 1977), I was firmly convinced that one should have a complete knowledge and understanding of the duck's anatomy before carving or painting a decoy. During my professional model building years, it was normal procedure to study the subject, review it over and over until it was totally clear, and then proceed with confidence. I have not changed my own carving procedure, but I have altered some beliefs for the benefit of those who want to jump right in and do it.

During the past several years I have met quite a few people who needed to begin carving before they lost interest. I could have warned them that once they started carving they would not have to worry about losing interest. Carving becomes a near-obsession for most who attempt it. I think novices should worry instead about losing their jobs, their spouses, their kids, or perhaps all of these. I have never been able to explain why the obsession occurs, but one thing is for sure—few escape it once caught up by carving fever.

In the hopes of fulfilling that need to jump right in, I have developed a very simple approach that will help build your confidence quickly. In *Wildlife in Wood,* I provided very little about how I would do something, letting the reader put it together a little at a time.

In this book, I have decided to show as much as I can to help you. Some people like to be shown how to do something before they attempt it. To satisfy this desire, I will show carving and painting step by step. It is my hope that you can at least get started in the right direction. This is very important because your first impressions are the most lasting impressions. If you start with the right understanding and correct methods, you can build the basics that will ensure your ultimate goal.

Anatomy of the Decoy

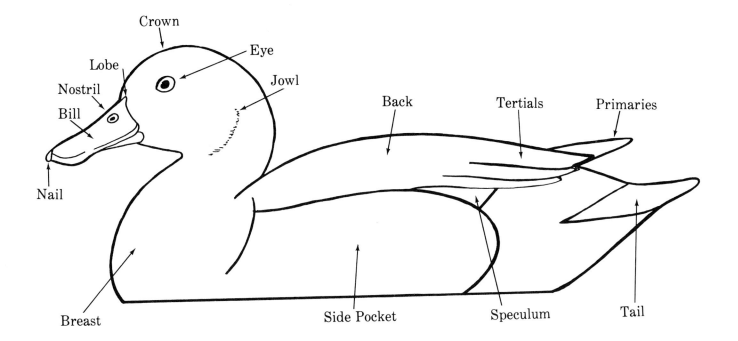

Author's Note

Readers will notice that various anatomical terms found in this book do not coincide with those used by ornithologists or biologists. I have renamed some areas of waterfowl anatomy so that laymen can associate them with known areas similar to other animals or objects with which they may already be familiar. In addition, terms and definitions are used to simplify their meanings to carvers and painters. I do not pretend to be trained as either an ornithologist or a biologist; this book was written solely to teach the techniques of reproducing wildfowl in wood as an art form.

Putting the Puzzle Together

Carving a decoy is very similar to putting a jigsaw puzzle together. Your introduction to puzzles was probably during childhood and the designs were very simple. The puzzles were made of large, easily recognized pieces. This simple design let you learn quickly and etched the shapes of the various pieces in your mind. As more of the puzzle was put together, it became easier to complete.

The first step in carving a decoy is similar to your earliest puzzles because it can be divided into large, simple pieces. The difference, however, is that the pieces have to be made. This step is *not* difficult if you know what the pieces should look like. I will outline the procedure in steps so you can mentally form the pieces and, then, physically carve them. As you progress to more complicated carvings, I will show why the various pieces of the puzzle are shaped the way they are.

Everything starts with a foundation or skeleton. If you try to progress too quickly, you might find yourself trying to put together a framework that will not fit on the foundation. Would your house fit on your neighbor's foundation? You are always better off building your own base or foundation so you can better understand the shape of the structure that has to fit it. It can never be too simple to start with. Remember that throughout the carving process and you will find learning easier. To keep my approach to carving simple, I will use some drawings instead of photographs. Thus, you should be able to isolate and concentrate on the most important aspects.

Miniature Mallard Decoy

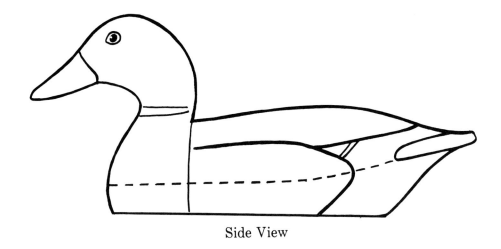

Side View

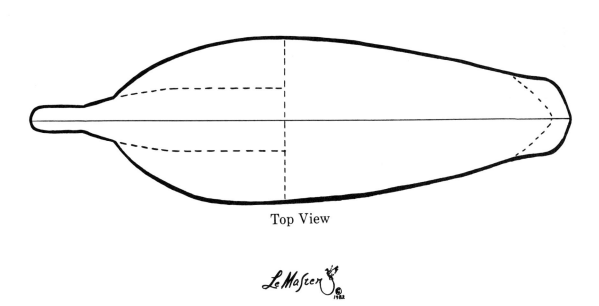

Top View

I have drawn this pattern to use for your first wooden decoy. It will not require enlarging or reducing as it is the actual size of the carving. In using the other patterns in this book, you will be on your own, but for now let's start the decoy.

The First Step

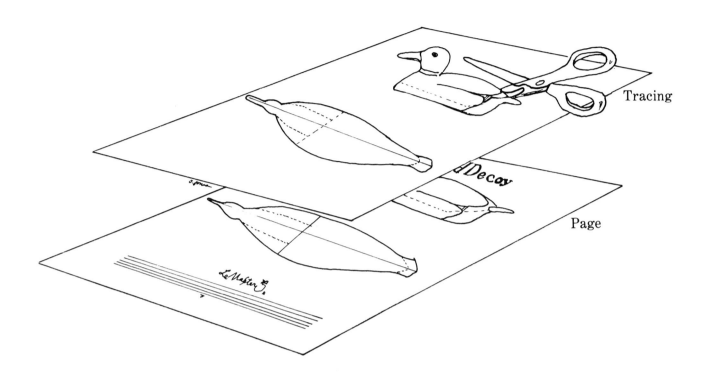

Trace all the lines of the pattern by using a transparent paper. Tracing paper is best, but you can also use wax paper with excellent results. After you have traced all the parts of the pattern, cut them out or transfer them to heavier paper or cardstock (use carbon paper) and then cut out. Save all patterns for future use and mark them with the species and the date.

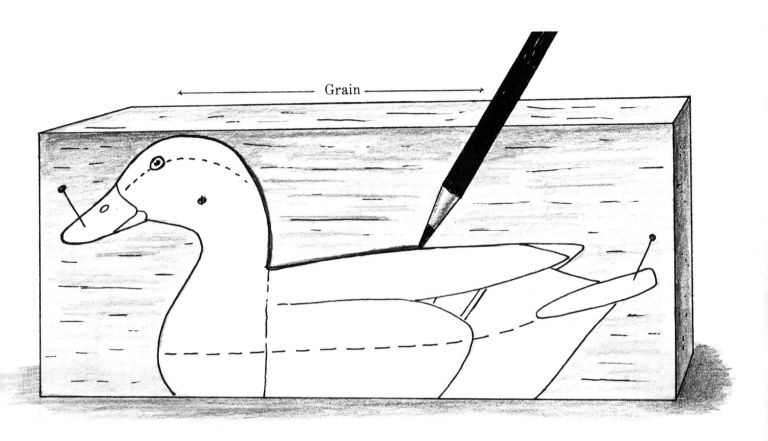

Make sure the grain runs the length of the wood before you start to mark the pattern on it.

Place the cutout pattern against the wood and line up the bottom of the pattern with the bottom of the wood. Use a pencil to outline the pattern onto the wood. Do not transfer all the lines of the pattern as they will all be cut away later—use the outline only.

Do not use felt tip markers on any carving—the ink will bleed through and ruin the final paint.

If you have trouble holding the pattern, pin it to the wood with straight pins.

After you have outlined the pattern, remove it and save it for some of the other steps.

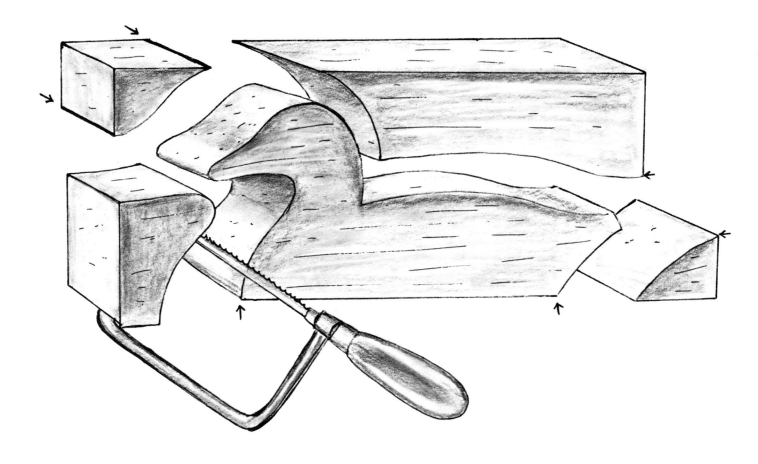

Once the outline is marked on the block of wood, the object is to cut away
everything that is on the outside of the pattern. In other words, get rid of
anything that doesn't look like a duck. The pattern can be reversed and traced
on the other side of the block. This will help you keep the cuts square with the
block.

To keep an accurate line for cutting, use a straight edge or a square and
mark lines across the block where the saw will enter and where you will finish
the cut (see arrows). Keep the saw in line with these lines as you cut the shape
from the wood. The best method is to use a jigsaw, band saw, or coping saw,
but if you don't have any of these available, a knife will do the job. If you use
a knife alone, approach it the same way as you would get ready to saw.
Remove the wood to the marked lines.

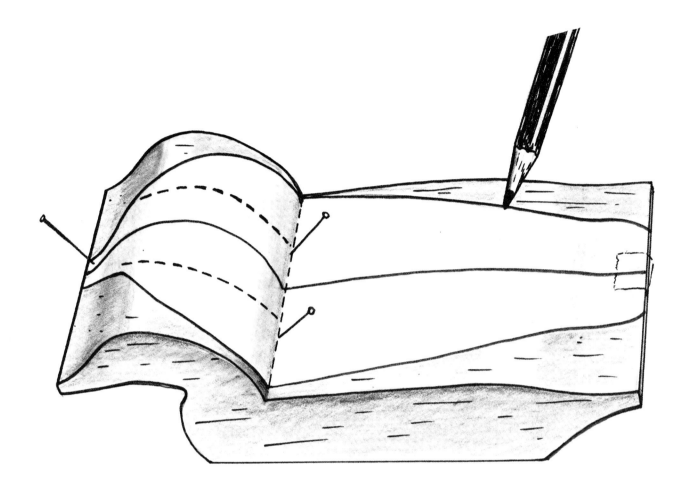

After cutting the side view from the block of wood, the next step is to cut out the top view using the top view pattern. Caution: *This pattern is designed to be placed over a specific contour that results from cutting out the side view first. Do not use it on the flat surface of the block before you carve the side view.*

Crease the pattern on the dotted line and place the fold in the crevice behind the neck. Use straight pins or tape to hold it in place. Once it is firmly positioned, trace all the lines onto the block, including the centerline and the outlines of the bod· ·nd head. If you have trouble tracing the inner lines, you can puncture the pattern and wood with a pin or knife and then mark the wood with pencil when the pattern is removed. You may have to hold the wood up to a strong light to see punctures.

After the pattern on the wood is complete, cut the outside edges away the same way you formed the side view.

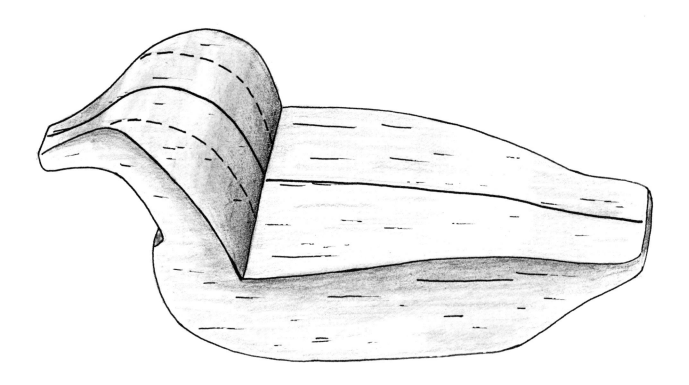

This is the shape you should have after cutting the patterns for the side and top. The centerline and the dotted lines for the head should be marked well so they will not be removed with handling. The centerline should be there until the final sanding.

Now is the time to bring the carving into better perspective. The area where the head is to be and its width has been marked. Cut the excess from each side of the head down to the dotted lines. (Compare this drawing with the previous one to see where the dotted lines were.) The wood should cut easily in this area if you use a downward motion and cut thin sections at a time.

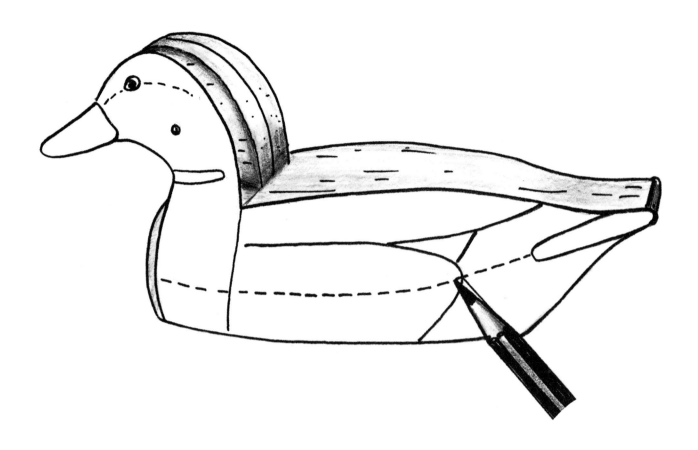

To ensure that the shape is not altered, a top centerline was established. To maintain the complete body shape, place the side pattern against the block again, which is now contoured, and trace or puncture the dotted line that angles from the front of the tail forward to the breast. The pattern will be shorter than the block due to the curvature of the body so line the pattern up at the tail and be sure to use this procedure on both sides of the block.

With both top and side centerlines in place, you now have established the exact perimeter of the carving. You will not have to cut into these lines for any of the remaining steps except in finishing touches. These lines will assure accuracy. All contours will be guided by these lines. This is similar to drawing a line over the top of a ball—it will always be the contour no matter how the ball is turned over.

Keeping the example of the ball in mind, the next step is to round the body. The rounding will begin from the lines on the side to the centerline on the top. The body is also rounded slightly from the centerlines of the side to the bottom. The upper area of the tail should remain somewhat flat, but it too may be rounded on the edges.

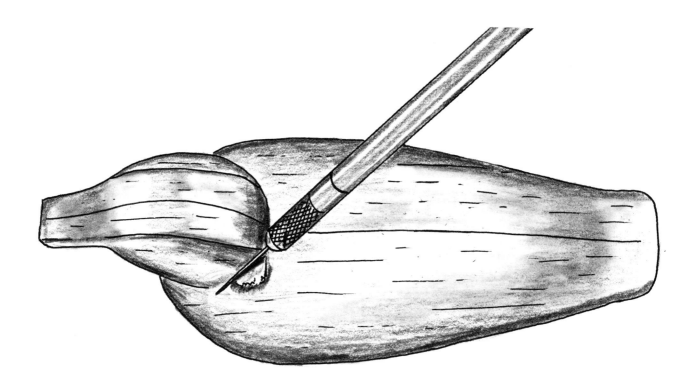

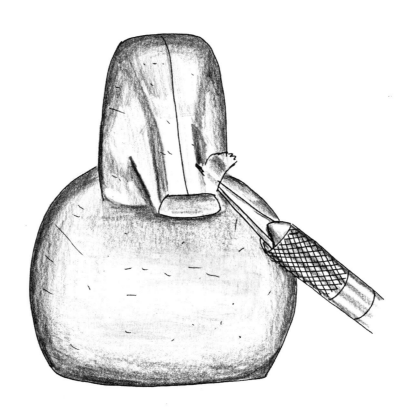

After satisfying yourself that the body of the carving is round, except for the flat bottom, you should begin to realize how easy it really is to carve a decoy.

Did you make sure to round the breast area?

If you have everything rounded on the body, the final shape of your carving will be attained by rounding the edges of the head and bill.

After you have it carved and rounded completely, sand it until it is smooth by using 150 grit sandpaper, then finishing it with 240 or 320 grit.

The final finish of the decoy is entirely up to you. The simplest method is to stain it and then seal it with varnish or lacquer. One of the easiest methods for your first carving is to use brown shoe polish and finish by buffing. However, you cannot paint over this later.

If you are more venturesome and want to paint the carving, you will need some extra aids. One of them is the painting guide that appears on page 20. You will need to trace and cut the pattern out if you are going to paint this miniature. The first step, though, is to seal the carving with white latex (interior house paint) or gesso from an art supply store. This also provides a consistent background for further painting. Both of these paints can be sanded lightly if you leave brush marks.

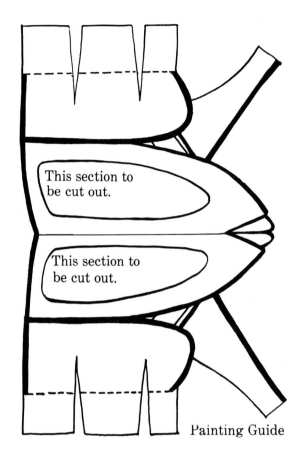

Painting Guide

At this point, your carving should be all white. After you have cut the painting guide out, turn it over and mark the lines with a soft-lead pencil—several times so you leave some lead on the paper.

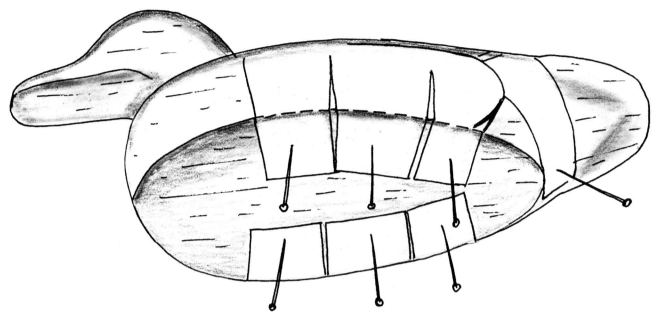

Once you have marked the underside of the guide, turn it back over and place it on the body and up against the neck. Wrap the guide around the body and pin or tape the tabs on the bottom. Make sure it is evenly spaced on both sides before securing.

Use a pencil and mark all the lines (including outlines) except the centerline on the back. If you press firmly enough, the lead that was left on the underside will act as a carbon and show up on the white paint. Make sure the lines are distinct enough to serve as guides before you remove the pattern.

Once the guide is removed, make sure that you remark the lines with pencil so you can preserve them as the carving is handled.

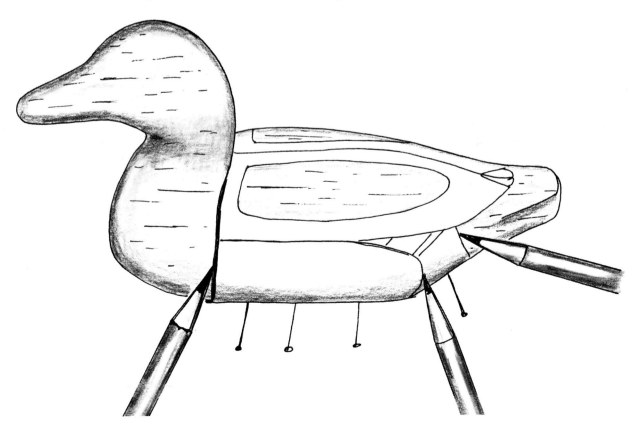

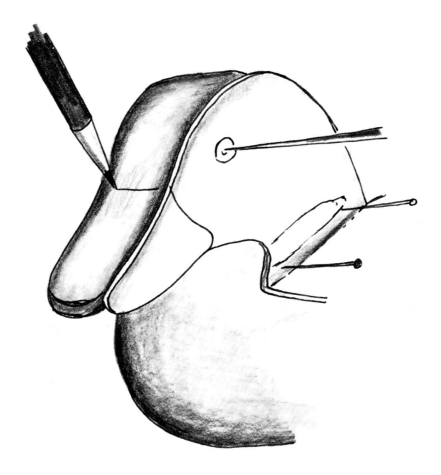

Fold the side-view pattern at the neck and line it up with the bill. Using it as a guide, mark the bill, eye, and the ring on the throat. Reverse the guide and do the same for the other side of the decoy. There is one minor area for you to mark on the top and bottom of the tail. Mark them as shown on the next drawing.

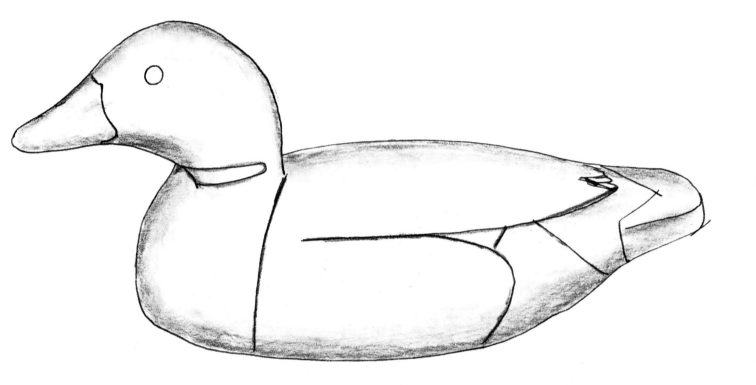

This drawing shows all the lines needed to guide you in painting the decoy. Instructions and colors for painting will be found in the sections on painting and in the color plates in the middle of this book.

    Painting your decoy will be as easy as carving if you take it one step at a time.

Remember my statement about the first puzzle? The more it was put together, the easier it became to do. Now would be a good time to put this decoy aside and carve another while the process is fresh in your mind. In fact, carving several of them would be better yet.

After you have mastered the basics, try some of the duck species on the following pages. No guides or instructions are included for these, so you will be on your own. Please note that the top views of these species cannot be used in the same way as the Mallard pattern.

Plans for Miniatures

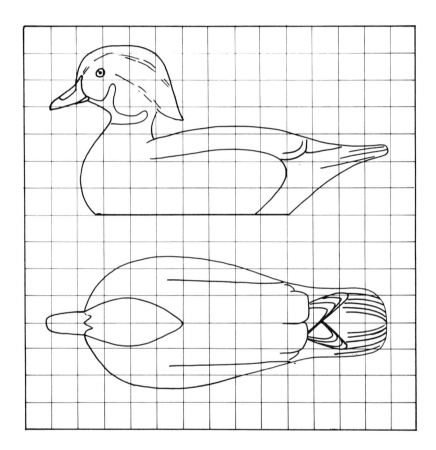

For full-scale decoys, enlarge squares to one inch.

Wood Duck

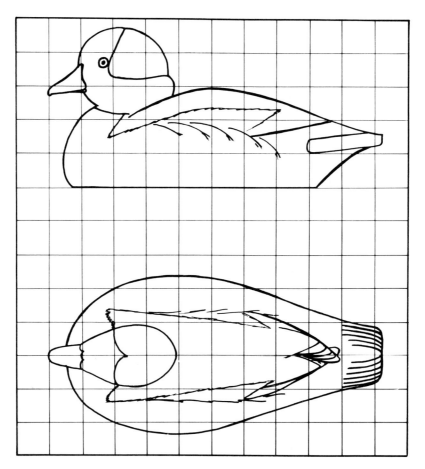

For full-scale decoys, enlarge squares to one inch.

Bufflehead

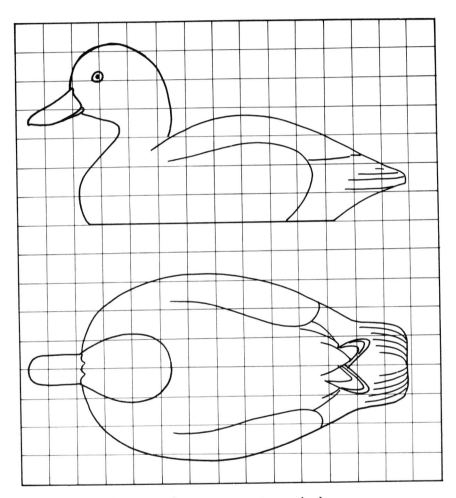

For full-scale decoys, enlarge squares to one inch.

Redhead

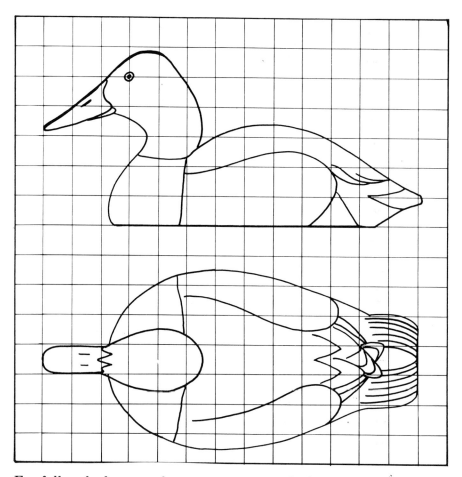

For full-scale decoys, enlarge squares to one inch.

Canvasback

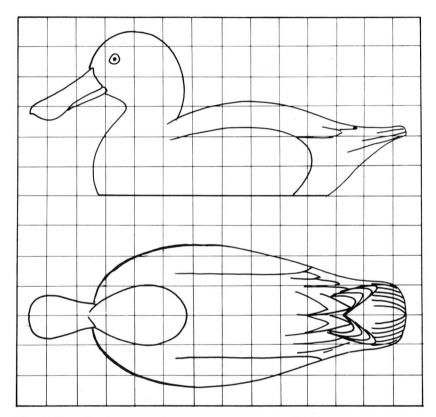

For full-scale decoys, enlarge squares to one inch.

Shoveler

For full-scale decoys, enlarge squares to ⅞ inch.

Green-winged Teal

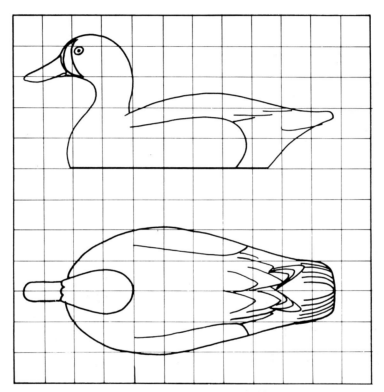

For full-scale decoys, enlarge squares to one inch.

Blue-winged Teal

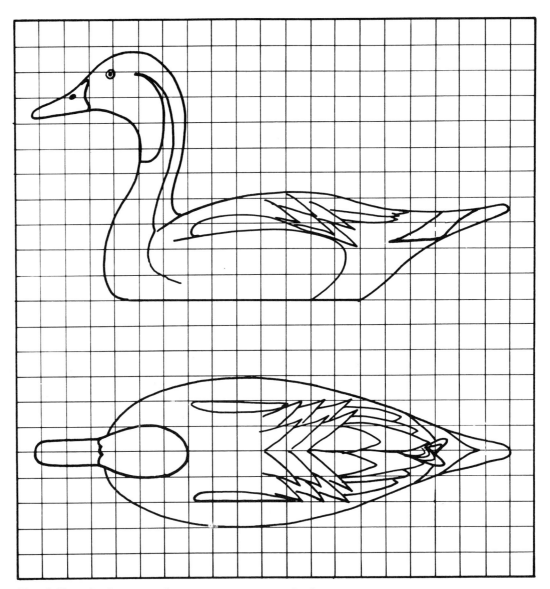

For full-scale decoys, enlarge squares to one inch.

Pintail

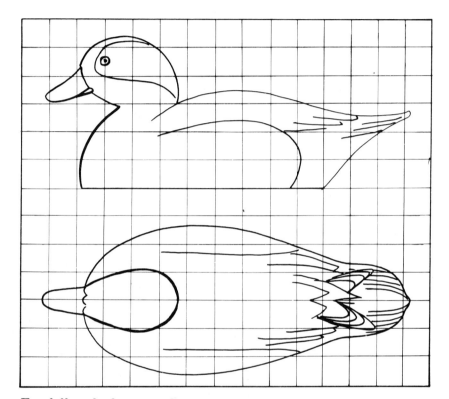

For full-scale decoys, enlarge squares to one inch.

Wigeon

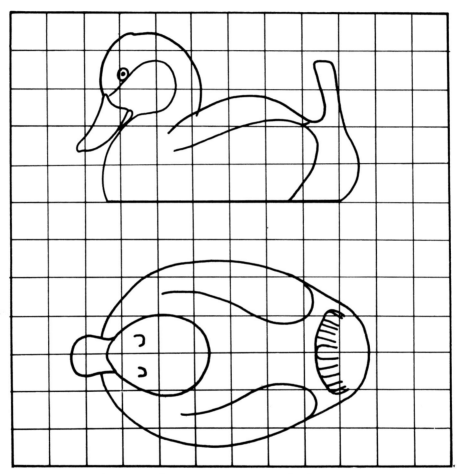

For full-scale decoys, enlarge squares to one inch.

Ruddy

Anatomy Axioms

I have developed a few axioms for anatomical features that can be applied to a large majority of ducks. There are exceptions to every rule, of course, but these will help you establish the proportions of the duck and the proper locations of its parts. Whenever you feel uneasy about the look on a particular carving, these axioms will help you reestablish the foundation.

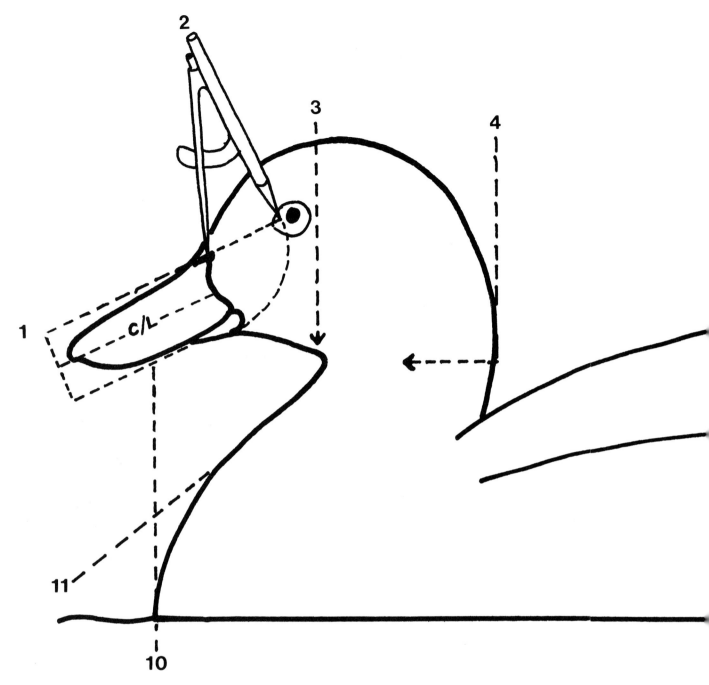

1. *The eye is located on a line extending through the top lobe of the bill. To find this line, box the general shape of the bill by establishing a centerline and extend the topline of the box to the rear.*

2. *Location of eye on the lobe line will be approximately the same distance as the bill is high.*

3. *The throat will be behind the eye (see broken vertical line).*

4. *The rearmost point of the head will be straight behind the throat.*

5. *The highest point of the back will be midway between the breast and the tail.*

6. *The tertials end just beyond the point where the tail starts.*

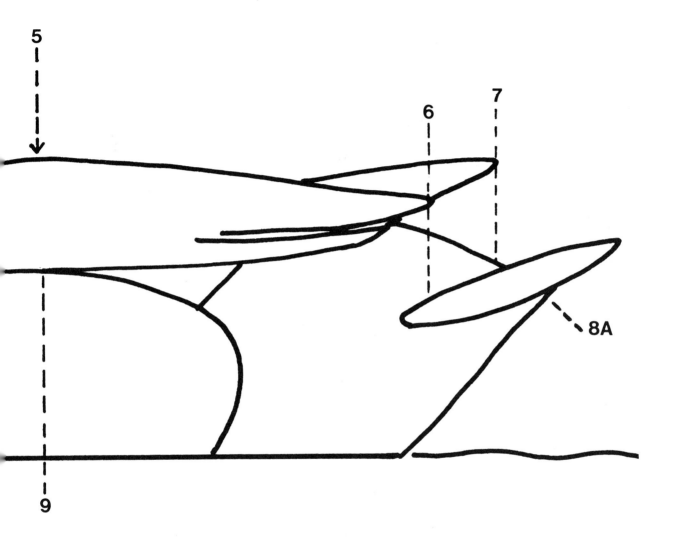

7. *The primaries normally extend to the midpoint of the tail (from a side view).*

8. *The tail angles upward on a relaxed duck.*

8A. *The body extends farther to the rear, underneath the tail, than on top.*

9. *The speculum starts approximately midway between breast and tail (if exposed).*

10. *One-half of the bill extends beyond the breast in the relaxed position.*

11. *The breast arcs gently from the throat to the waterline.*

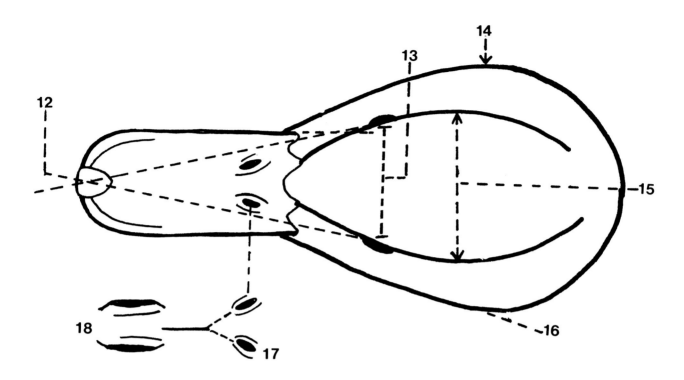

12. *Viewed from above, the eyes create an angle that points at the end of the nail.*

13. *The distance between the eyes cannot be closer to each other than the width of the bill at the head, though they can be wider.*

14. *The jowl forms the widest area of the head.*

15. *The width of the crown will be more than half the width of the head.*

16. *The shape of the head is established by the line from the bill to the jowl.*

17. *The nostrils of puddle ducks angle in toward the nail.*

18. *The nostrils of diving ducks are relatively parallel to each other.*

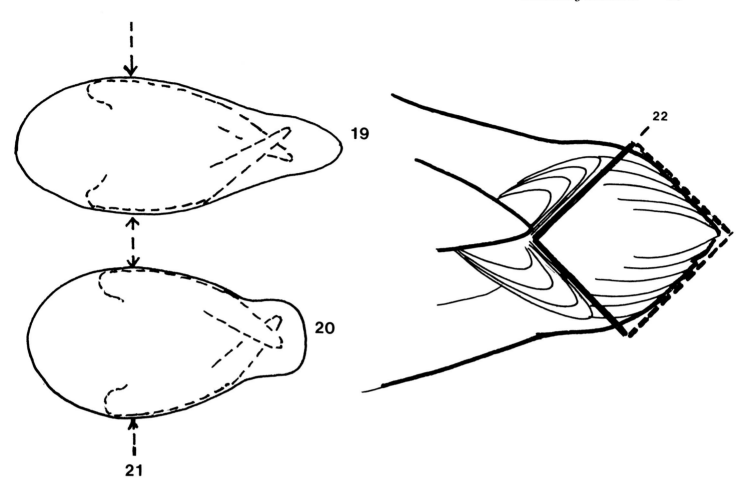

19. The body shape of puddle ducks resembles a long teardrop.

20. The body shape of diving ducks resembles a chunky teardrop.

21. The duck's body is widest where the wings push the sidepocket out.

22. The flatter side of the primaries is on the inside. Remember a diamond or box shape and use the primaries to form two sides.

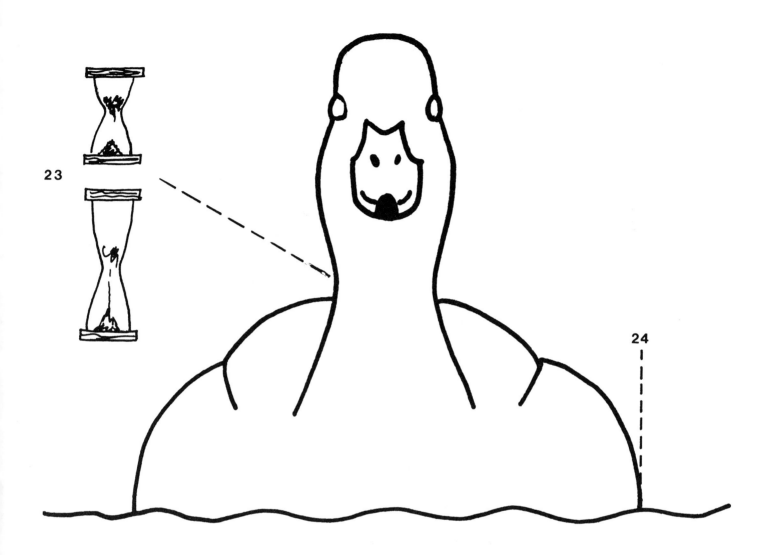

23. *From the front, the neck resembles an hourglass shape. The head at the jowl tapers to the throat and widens again from the throat to the breast. With head raised high it resembles a tall hourglass.*

24. *The body shape starts tapering inward from the waterline.*

Observing the Flaws

Flaws, mistakes, errors—whatever you wish to label them—have plagued me from the time I built my first model airplane as a youngster. If I should ever eliminate them completely, however, I would probably quit carving, for it is likely that the challenges they offer are what keeps me going.

I was fortunate while growing up: A ten-cent kit and a nickel tube of glue were my rewards for watching my two brothers while my mother and father were at work. Each week, I completed a new model airplane and immediately hid it before someone could see the flaws—the mistakes I had made. When others did see my models, they invariably told me they were magnificent, but I knew better. They had *flaws*. It was a real challenge to overcome these flaws, especially when no one else was available to help or to give guidance. After many years of model building, I developed the ability to observe and detect imperfections. Of course, the "oohs" and "aahs" of those who saw my models helped encourage me to go on.

This early experience set directions for my entire life and so I adopted this simple maxim: *Look for the flaws first, eliminate them one by one, and then there will be beauty.* A vast majority of people are so struck by beauty or what they perceive as beauty that they rarely see flaws that a trained observer will see.

Nothing is perfect, but we often tend to settle for flawed products because we are dazzled by superficial brilliance. My search for flaws has been very frustrating and yet perhaps more rewarding than most people would realize. We need to look past the brilliant first impression, to find and eliminate the flaws and let the beauty emerge slowly. As the imperfections are modified one by one, we can then see the work of art as it really should be.

To detect imperfections you must be able to observe. How many times have you heard, "You must observe something before you really see it"? Observation is an ability or talent to concentrate and isolate parts of what you see. Observation lets you perceive the whole of what you see but breaks it down like a jigsaw puzzle, piece by piece, section by section, area by area, color by color, size by size, etc. You put things together when you observe, they are already together when you see.

It is relatively easy to train yourself to observe flaws by concentrating until it becomes second nature for you. We all use these powers of observation every day at work and in leisure pursuits. From detecting typing errors in the office to finding loose bolts on the machinery in the field, we use observation to correct flaws as we work. In reality, you are observing as you read this page; you are concentrating on each word or you could not read them. Yet vision permits you to see the whole page and, perhaps, other parts of your surroundings as well. Reading is one of the strongest examples of observation. All the while you are reading, you are mentally obliterating everything except that which you wish to observe.

We have all developed an ability to observe in our chosen interests (job, hobbies, household tasks). But what does one do when entering a new area? I have developed a simple method that allows you to block off or eliminate everything that is not needed at a particular stage of production until we get to the next stage. To do this you can create a mask that can be used to view only one thing at a time until you get used to observing immediately what you should be looking for.

Making and Using the Mask

Lay the mask over a picture or even the wooden decoy just completed. The hole may have to be larger or smaller, depending on the size of the subject under study. The hole can be square, round, or oblong as long as it is designed to fit your needs. By moving the mask from area to area, closely scrutinize each detail. The mask will let you focus only on one particular part without being dazzled by the brilliance of the whole.

Common Decoy Flaws

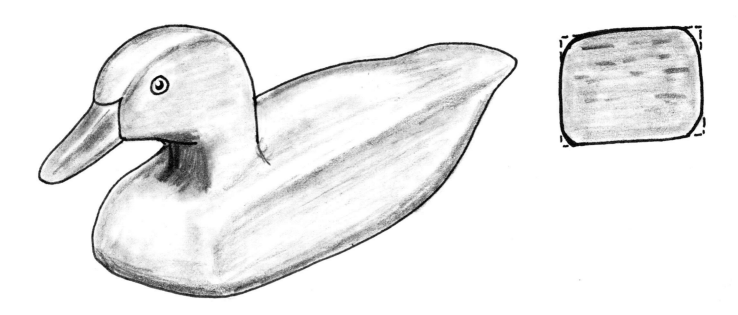

The square decoy—the flat sides and top indicate that the carver was afraid of taking too much off, was lazy and didn't want to work any harder, or didn't know that ducks are round.

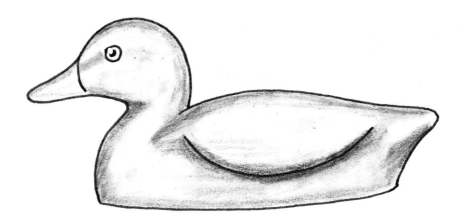

Having the wing on the outside usually means the carver followed a taxidermist's mount or didn't know that there is a sidepocket for it to fit into. A swimming duck normally keeps its wings tucked away for protection.

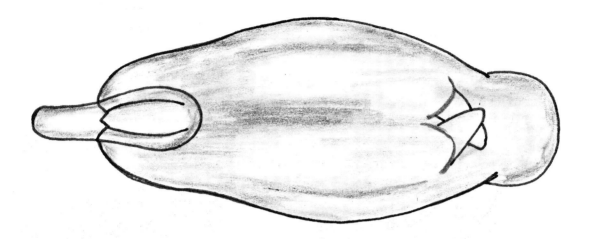

Narrow breast and wide rear body—Viewed over the shoulder from behind, a live duck will give the illusion of this shape. When seen from directly above, the body resembles a full teardrop shape with a tail attached.

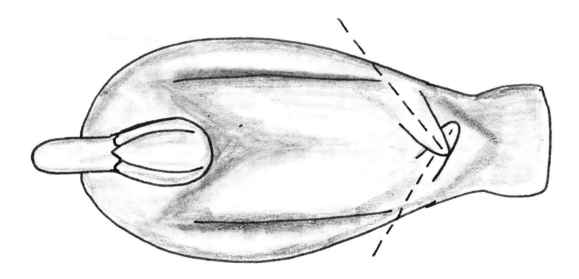

Wing direction—Even though the wings are tucked under the feathers and only the tips show, you still have to convey the fact that they extend or point to the widest spot on the body (the point at which they push the sidepocket out). The tips cannot go off to the sides or straight up the middle.

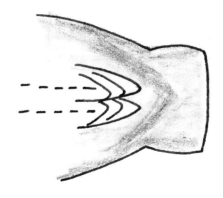

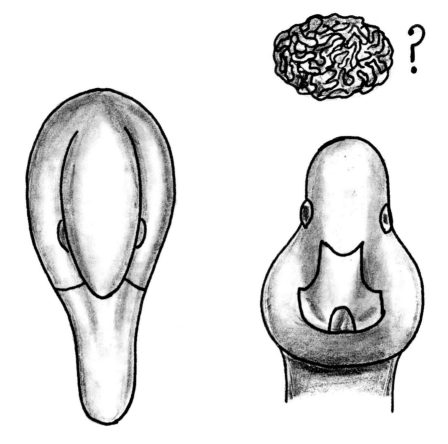

The most common flaw (left) *is to carve the bill to meet the head. Except on a couple of species, the bill does not flare outward at the head. The head shape contours to meet the bill, not vice versa.*

Room for brains? Although ducks are not known for their intelligence, they do have brains. A common error (right) *is to carve a narrow pinhead-looking duck because the carver forgot to leave room for the brain.*

The strangled decoy—Rarely does a duck exhibit a hoselike neck. It tapers into an hourglass shape, although not as severely from the side as from the front.

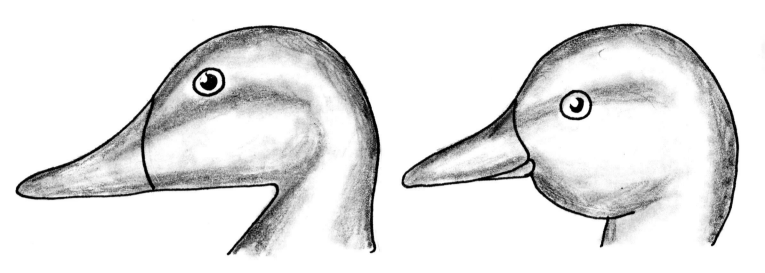

Extending the flatness of the bill to the head, or bulging the underside seems to indicate that the carver was not interested in observing the true shape of a live duck.

Shown are four different eye placements—Use the axioms given on pages 35 and 49 to pick out the right one. Or is the correct placement apparent?

The Eyes Have It

Without the eyes there is nothing to connect the decoy to a living object. The eyes give life to inanimate objects. Without them such objects can only resemble the form or shape of that object. If you doubt this observation, cover the eye of an animal or bird in any picture you may find, including photographs. If the photograph was taken while the bird or animal was in motion, the eye usually has an intense stare. Although the photograph is taken of a fraction of a second, there is still a feeling of the movement about to happen because of the intensity of the eyes. Cover the eye in the picture and the feeling of movement disappears. The animal or bird will then have a statuesque appearance only, frozen for eternity in a movement that will never be completed. Uncover the eyes and the feeling or warmth of living returns.

The use of eyes on the decoy is the single most important aspect of your carving. If the eyes are not properly positioned, the whole concept may be destroyed. There is a definite location of the eyes on the head. I have presented this information before but it is so important to the outcome of the carving that it is worth repeating.

Axiom for Eye Location

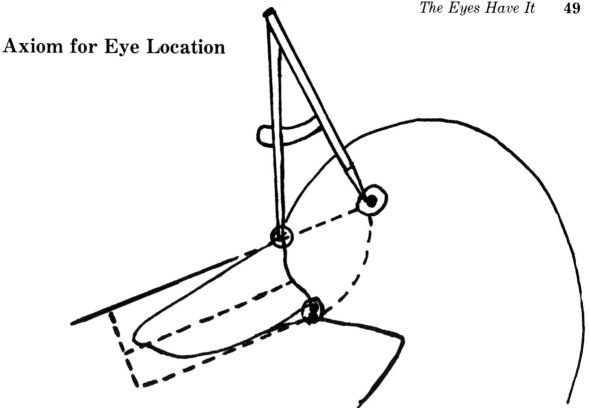

The top corners of the bill, at the point where they meet the head, are what I call the lobes of the bill. The eye is located on a straight line from the top lobe. To find the correct angle of the line, box in the overall appearance of the bill and extend the topline toward the back of the head. This centerline of the eye is bisected by another line—the eye is a distance from the bill that is equal to the height of the bill at the head. This normally includes the top and bottom parts of the bill. This measurement will mark a spot that will be in the front half of the eye. The actual center will be slightly beyond the intersection of the two lines.

Study this diagram. Once you understand the principles of finding the eye's location you should have no trouble in positioning the eyes on any of your decoys.

The eyes also angle or slant toward the front (see axioms). Keep in mind that the bird has to see to eat. Waterfowl have both binocular and monocular vision. Looking with both eyes is termed binocular. However, when they look forward with both eyes they can see only a few feet ahead, because both eyes have minimal focusing ability. Anything beyond a few feet has to be viewed with only one eye, hence such viewing with one eye is termed monocular. The duck has to turn its head to the side to do so, but it is better able to see at great distance.

If you have ever tried to photograph ducks and waited impatiently for a front view, you would understand this better. A duck rarely presents a head-on view if it is aware of your presence. This posture would limit the duck's vision and thereby increase the danger to it.

The Eye Trough

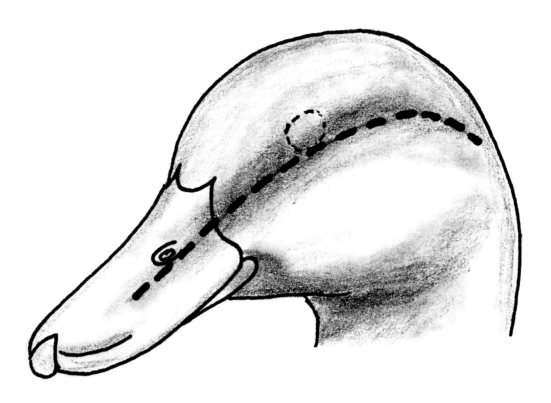

A depression or trough extends both forward and backward from the eye so vision is not blocked. Like humans, ducks also have to be able to look down their nose (bill) without having their vision obstructed as they eat. A duck can also see to the rear, although this ability is more limited than forward vision. The eye can be tilted slightly to see overhead as well.

One thing is for certain—most of the time, the eyes are not parallel (i.e., set flat on each side of the head).

Ducks do not have upper eyelids as humans do. Eyelids are on the bottom and close upward. Ducks' eyes do not have tearducts, but have nictitating membranes that protect the eyes and keep them moist. These membranes close from the front to the rear of the eye. Waterfowl do not blink their eyes as humans do; the membranes swipe the eyes to retain moisture. The nictitating membranes also protect the eyes and cover them when the duck is in danger or underwater, or when there is inclement weather. They fold in the front of the eye, creating corners similar to the tearduct corners of human eyes. The nictitating membranes are not something you would try to show on a decoy, but knowing that they are there should help you create the shape of the eyes.

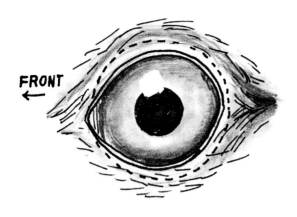

FRONT

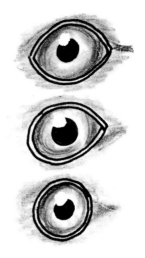

The correct shape of the exposed portion of eye. The dotted line represents perimeter of the glass eye.

Mistakes often made with eye shape on decoys.

Using highly rounded glass eyes or setting the eyes at wrong depth may create a bug-eyed look to your decoy.

Eye Alignment Guide

A frequent problem with the decoy's eyes is misalignment. Placing one eye higher than, or behind, the other happens more often than we would like to admit, especially if you do not have a drill press and the block was drilled before carving. If you are one of the many who has alignment difficulty, perhaps this eye guide (below left) *will help.*

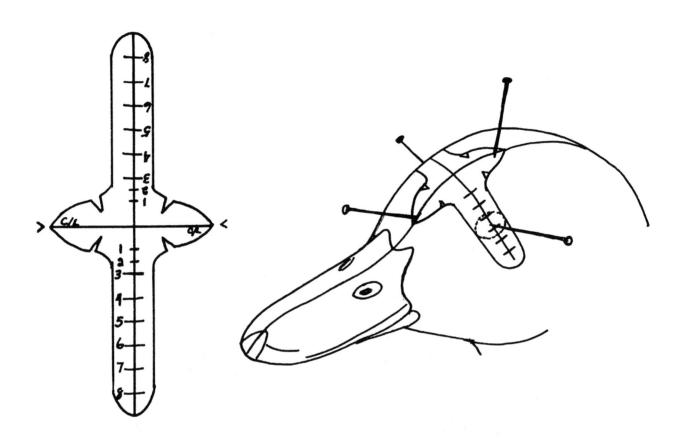

The first step in the use of the eye alignment guide is to locate one eye by using the axioms.

Next, looking straight down on the top of the head, mark a centerline (above right) *from the bill to the back of the head. Be as accurate as you can with the centerline and sight measure.*

Once the centerline is established, place the guide pointers on the line and bend the long tabs over the head. Move the guide backward or forward until you have the centerline of the long tab lined up with the center of the eye. Pin or tape it in place when you have everything in line.

Using the crosshatch marks as a means of measuring, mark the opposite tab the same distance from the top centerline to the center of the first eye. Bend the second tab over the head and locate the opposite eye by puncturing the tab at the same location as the first.

Setting Eyes

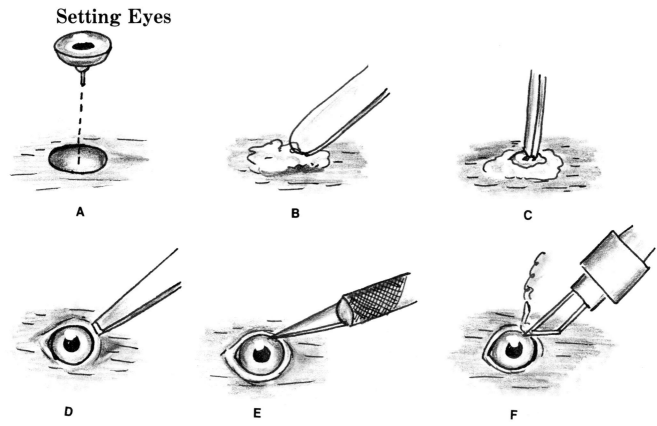

A.   Drill a hole slightly larger than the diameter of the glass eye. Make sure the glass eye will slip easily in and out of the hole and that it is deep enough to hold the eye. After you have the setting material in the hole is a poor time to find out that the eye is too big for the hole you drilled.

B.   Work the setting material thoroughly into the wood. The dust of the wood can be worked into the material without ill effect.

C.   Push the eye into the setting material with a piece of wood. Remove the excess material as it is pushed out around the edges. Now is the time to make sure of the placement, the depth, and the angle of the eye.

D.   Using a piece of wood, form the edges and contour of the eye. Remove material if needed or rebuild if necessary.

E.   After the material has set, trim it with a knife and then file or sand the contours around the eye. Do not touch the glass with file or sandpaper.

F.   I find it easy to remove unwanted materials by using one of my woodburners. The heat destroys the material and it will flake off easily. However, *DO NOT USE HEAT ON THE ONE-DROP, SUPER GLUES.*

Eyes can be put in or set with any material that will adhere to the wood and harden. One type may be easier for you to work with than another, so you may have to experiment until you find one you are comfortable working with. The most commonly used materials for setting eyes are plastic wood, wood putty, acrylic modeling compound, automotive body filler, ribbon epoxy, five-minute epoxy, and plastic lead. At first, some of these may solidify or harden faster than you are capable of working. If this should happen, most of these materials can be trimmed with a knife. If it is too hard to work with, a woodburner can be used to heat the material and flake it off easily. Be careful, though, and do not apply heat directly to the glass eye; it will crack if it gets too hot. Do not be afraid to dig the eye out and reset it if you are not satisfied with your results.

Helpful Hints

If you have trouble finding glass eyes, check with your local taxidermist.

If you should scratch a glass eye, apply clear fingernail polish to the entire surface. The scratch will not be noticed.

Instead of painting the clear eyes, you can color them by mixing the eye color (powdered pigment) into the setting material. When the entire mass of the setting agent is the right color, it will act as a backing for the glass. Also, by precoloring the setting material you will not have to worry about the paint lifting from the back of the eye. Acrylics or oil colors normally cannot be used to color the setting material because they will not mix.

Dark colors mixed with the setting material will cause it to solidify or harden much more quickly than normal. I use this to my advantage when I don't wish to hold things for long periods waiting for the material to harden.

If you paint the back of the eyes with acrylic colors, coat it also with five-minute epoxy. Applied over the paint, it will keep it from lifting or reacting from the setting material.

Plastic wood or wood putty may attack any acrylic paint on the back of the eye.

Automotive body filler may generate too much internal heat as it cures and may cause the paint to lift from the rear of the glass eye. Use less hardener if this problem occurs.

If any of the automotive body fillers are used and the material stays spongy and not hard, you have used too much hardening agent. There is a point at which more hardener just makes the plastic softer and does not hasten the curing.

Make sure the black pupils are approximately the same size on the same carving. Although both eyes normally will not be viewed at the same time, they should look similar from each side.

Wood

The woods used most widely for carving decoys are basswood, cedar, pine, jelutong (imported), tupelo, and cypress. However, you can order and buy almost any type of wood in the world if you know who or where the suppliers are. Until you have experience with carving and have used different types of wood obtained locally, however, you should not be concerned with ordering unknown woods. At first, use whatever is available.

Small lumberyards are not usually good places to look for carving wood. Some lumberyards may carry thicker wood stock and various types of wood, but in general they will have only thinner redwood or clear pine. Thin boards can be glued together to form larger blocks for carving, and are acceptable substitutes, but by no means are they the best for decoy carving. When there are many glue joints, some of them are likely to show on the finished carving. Any time two pieces of wood are glued together, even from the same board, expansion and contraction can occur due to moisture combined with heat and cold. If the wood is well sealed, these changes will be minimal, that is, as long as the wood had a low-moisture content at the time it was sealed. The ideal is to buy kiln-dried wood. Kiln-dried wood has been heated to dry out the moisture content. Naturally, it is more expensive because of the extra time and work involved. A good piece of kiln-dried lumber can be many times as expensive as one that is not.

I have had the opportunity to buy basswood at fifty cents per board foot, turned it down, and bought kiln-dried basswood for three dollars per board foot. The cheaper wood was not stable in moisture content and it might have created a risk for me; risk in the sense that it might dry out and crack long after I had finished carving it. The difference between the two prices was insurance that my clients would not have to call me in a year or so and say, "Guess what happened?" If your carvings are to be first class—you have to start with first-class wood.

While on vacation in the Bahamas a few years ago, I had a chance to purchase one of the local woodcarvings. It was beautifully done (even if the subject had six toes on each foot) and the price was affordable. Several months after I got it home—and safely, I might add—a small crack appeared in the bottom. Before the crack stopped expanding, it extended from bottom to top and eventually split in half. The Bahamanian native had used freshly cut wood and was not concerned that I might bring it back.

Where to Get Wood

Most metropolitan areas have hardwood supply centers that can be good sources for you. If you live out in the boonies like me, check local sawmills. Check the Yellow Pages under "Wood Products" or "Woodworking." Check with the businesses listed and ask for carving wood. If they do not have what you want, ask if they can recommend a source or give you some suggestions. Most woodworkers are usually very helpful.

If you get wood from local suppliers such as sawmills, ask if it has been air or kiln dried. It does not have to be kiln dried; air-dried wood is very acceptable as long as it was cured properly and the moisture content is below 10 percent.

An alternative to buying wood is to cut your own. Of course, you have to find someone that will let you have the tree for cutting. If you should cut your own, treat (cure) it properly before carving. Books that will show the particulars of treating wood are available at your local library.

Marv Meyer from Richfield, Minnesota, sent me notes on his methods for drying his own wood. He uses hardwoods extensively, but his methods should work for all kinds. The following drawings show how you can do it.

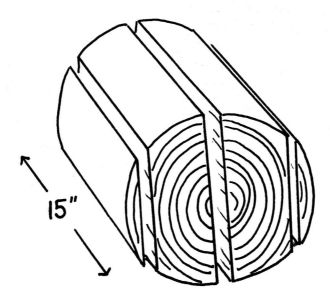

First, using a chain saw, he cuts the log into lengths of approximately 15 inches. The next cut is made down the center of each cut piece. It is important to make the center cut first, *he says. After the center cut, he cuts down both sides, leaving two thick pieces and the two smaller edge pieces.*

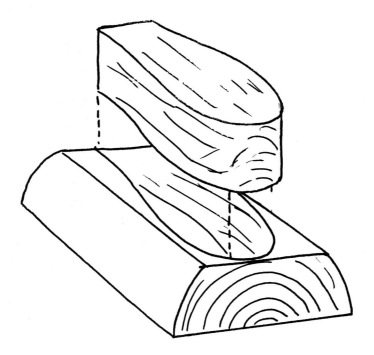

Marv then draws a pattern on each of the thicker sections and cuts them out with a band saw. This is just a rough pattern and not intended as a final outline for a carving.

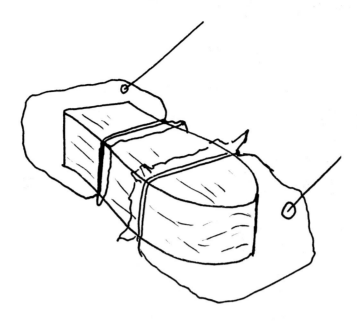

The last step is to put a plastic bag on each end of the rough-shaped blocks. Use rubber bands to hold the bag in place. Cut a hole in each of the bags to let the moisture out slowly as the wood dries. The size of the hole should be about the size of a dime or smaller, so the wood will not dry too quickly and crack.

To cure the wood, Marv stores these rough-cut blocks among the rafters in his garage during the summer months. Even in Minnesota the temperature in the rafters will reach 110–120 degrees in the summer. This heat will reduce the moisture content to acceptable levels. Without the heat, it would take several years to reduce the moisture to 10 percent.

I have been told that it takes one year for each inch of thickness for lumber to air dry—even if properly sealed on the ends.

Another suggestion came from Marv; one that I believe is an excellent idea, but should be tried at your own risk. He has dried small pieces of wood in the microwave using the *defrost cycle*. A seven-inch piece of butternut or walnut takes him about 30 minutes to cure. There are, however, precautions that must be taken before placing the wood in the microwave.

Microwave Curing

The wood should be shaped first. Then drill a ⅜-inch hole in the neck from the top side and a series of smaller holes at angles in the bottom of the shape. The holes allow steam to escape from the wood as it dries. Without the holes the wood will pop like a kernel of popcorn, Marv states. He also places a glass of water in the microwave with the wood so the machine will not be damaged when the moisture content of the wood is eliminated. Marv has had success with this method, but I URGE YOU TO DO IT WITH CAUTION—check your oven's manual of operation—AND AT YOUR OWN RISK.

When Buying Lumber

You may be stymied if you order lumber and the salesperson asks if you want 4-, 6-, or 8-quarter lumber. Wood other than the lumberyard variety is sold by thickness measured in quarter-inch increments. If you want wood with a one-inch thickness, you would ask for 4/4, meaning 4 times ¼ of one inch. If you wish 1½-inch thickness, it would be termed 6/4, 2-inch is 8/4, 3-inch is 12/4, and 4-inch is 16/4. If you have any doubts about this, lay it out with a ruler before you order. If you should get the wrong size, you will wish that you had taken the time to understand it.

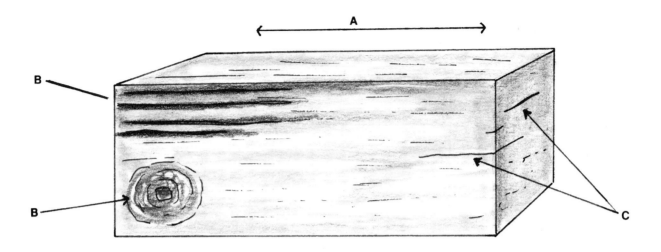

A. *Look for grain running the length of the wood.*

B. *Try to find wood with close grain and no vivid markings (knots)
in the grain.*

C. *Watch for cracks; they may be hairline small but will enlarge in time.*

*If you use a water-soluble glue to join two or more pieces of wood together,
dampen both pieces with a wet sponge before applying the glue. This will let
the glue disperse more evenly and will lessen buildup. Clamp the wood until
dry.*

Tools

I wish I had a few simple suggestions concerning tools. Many books are available on tools and how to use them. It would be foolish to think that I could cover this subject in a few pages—especially when you are probably more concerned with *how* to carve decoys than what to carve them with.

Tools used to achieve excellent results for some carvers create havoc for others. Carving tools are extensions of the carver's hands. Most avid carvers have favorite tools—try to talk them into using anything else and you better be ready for an argument.

There isn't any doubt that you should have a saw. The blocking out of the patterns can be done with a regular handsaw if necessary. You may decide to use a coping saw, hacksaw, jigsaw, saber saw, or the ultimate, the band saw, but none of these are necessities.

Blocks can also be cut and shaped with a hatchet. Any tool that removes the wood will do. I have said many times that a fingernail file or an emery board will do. It may take longer to carve with these simple tools, but they will do the job with your guidance.

There are many types of knives that will cut the wood very efficiently, including drawknives, hunting knives, pocket knives, paring knives, butcher knives, and carving knives. Each will remove wood as well as any of the others as long as it is sharpened properly. Other tools that remove wood are rasps, files, riflers, sandpaper, gouges, and chisels. If your budget allows, you can expedite the job mechanically with flexible shaft machines, rotary machines, hand machines, and grinders. There is something for everyone—the problem lies in making an initial choice. If I had to make this choice, knowing what I do about carving and faced with budget problems, I would start with a saw; rasp; a small, razor knife; and sandpaper. These would get me a good start until I had enough experience to determine my actual needs.

The Full-Size Decoy

The miniature decoy was relatively easy to carve; a full-size decoy is no different, just larger. There will be more wood to handle and to remove, but the basics are the same. To further the challenge, therefore, I have not included the helpful guide patterns used for marking the miniature. This time I will show the carving procedure through photographs. (Now is the time to start practicing the art of observing.)

Bufflehead Drake Decoy

I have chosen the Bufflehead drake because of its simplicity and its distinctive features. It is also one of the easiest ducks to paint.

The first step in making the full-size decoy is to enlarge the pattern shown here by marking a graph of one-inch squares, then complete the outlines of the two views of the decoy. It will be a full-sized pattern when you are finished. This can be done for all the patterns on pages 25–34. Cut the pattern out and mark the species and date on all pieces of the pattern. Patterns frequently get mixed, but are easily separated *if* marked.

Bufflehead Drake Decoy

Bufflehead Drake Decoy

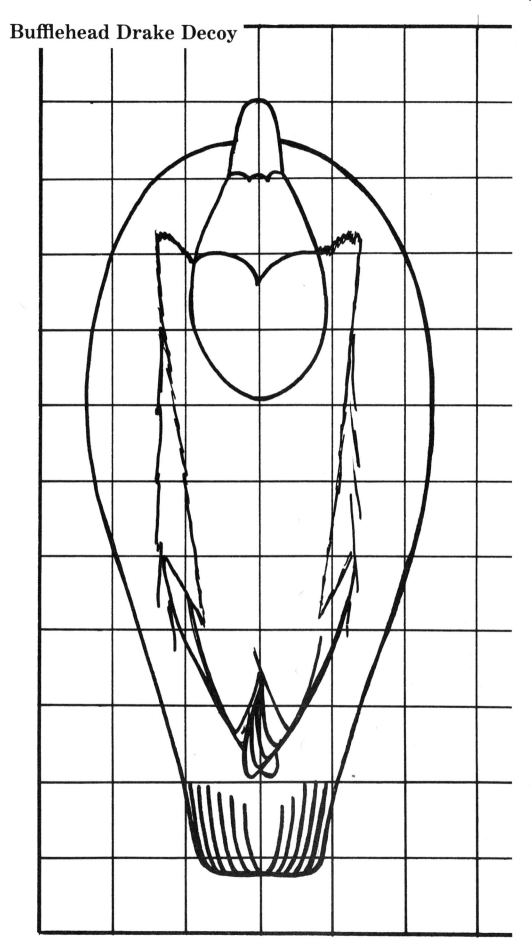

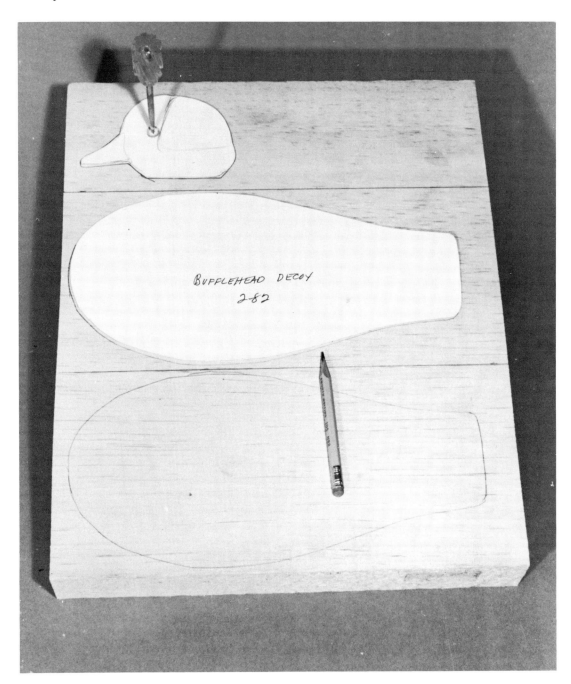

The top view pattern is to be placed on the flat board for this decoy (unlike the miniature, which used the side view first). If the wood you are using is three or more inches thick, you will have to mark only one pattern. If you have to glue pieces together, mark the pattern on each piece. The head is to be carved separately for this decoy; therefore, mark the pattern for it as well. If you have a drill press, you can predrill the eye location after the head shape is cut out. Cut the body shape (top view) when you have the pattern completed.

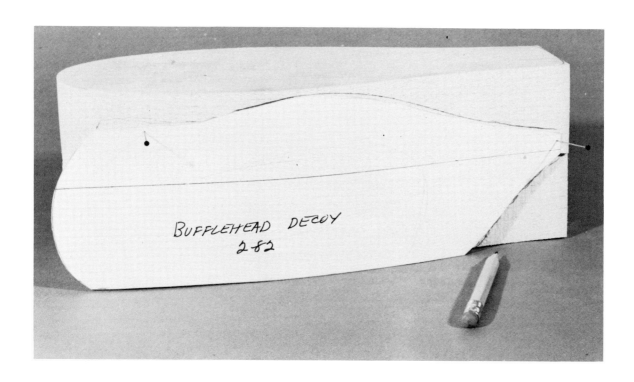

Stack the pieces (not glued as yet) and mark the side pattern. The blocks are contoured, so you will not be able to wrap the pattern around it without distortion. Sight-measure the front part of the pattern and mark the blocks. Pins will help hold the pattern in place and free both hands for measuring and marking.

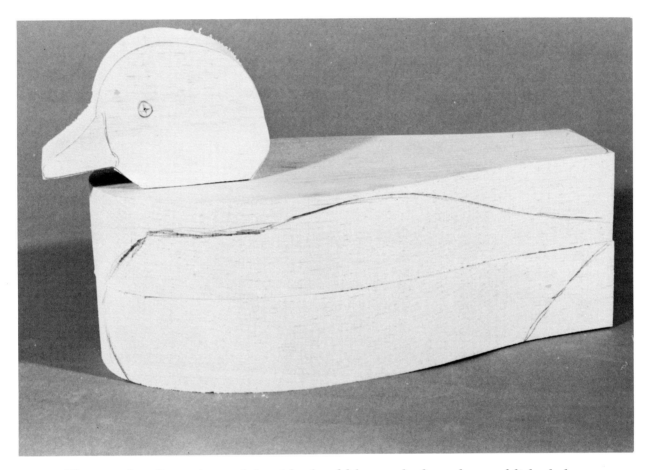

The exterior dimensions of the side should be marked on the established shape (top view). Place all three pieces together for visual check. The head will be lower when the side view is cut out.

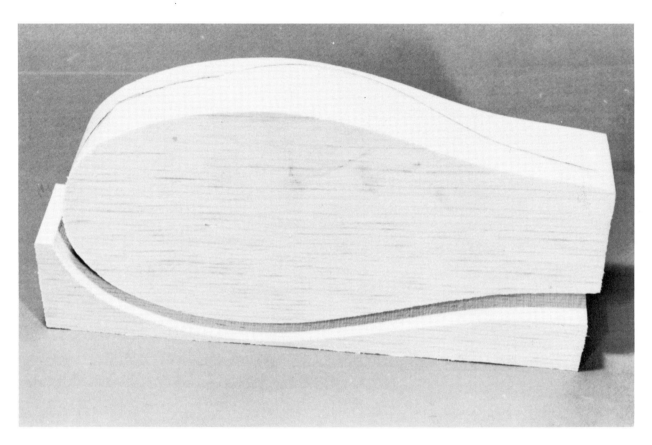

One of the cutoffs from the top view pattern should be used to solidify the block as it is sawn out.

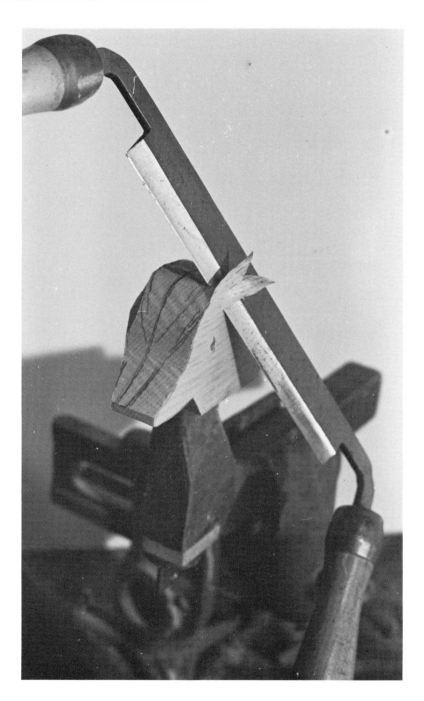

I usually start carving the head first. If I have trouble getting it right, I'll do another. It is the eyes, then the head that give character, so you have to get them right. Establishing the centerline first, mark the bill outline and then the head outline. Shape the head to these dimensions. You do not have to use a drawknife as shown in these pictures.

After the basic head shape is carved, establish and cut the eye trough. I used a gouge for this but a knife will work just as well.

It is easier to finish shaping the head with a rasp than to carve it with a knife. It will also help smooth the surface of the carving cuts.

Make sure the head fits flat on the body. In this case carving was needed to flatten the surface. The head will be held with a screw (besides glue) so a hole was drilled in the center of the area where the head has been marked.

With the head resting in place and both blocks stacked but not glued, the top centerline should be established. The side curvature line should also be marked at this time, but without using the pattern. You are on your own this time.

I decided to hollow the decoy, but it needed to be shaped first. The old-timers held the pieces of a decoy together with screws; I use automotive body filler, which is an excellent adhesive. The problem with this lies in separating the pieces. To accomplish this, circle troughs should be cut into the block with a small spot left in the center of each. The body filler should be rubbed into the two spots and the top section put in place. Let the body filler set and cure before the next step.

A scrap block of wood can be screwed to the bottom of the decoy so that it can be clamped into the vise. A drawknife can be used to remove the excess wood and to round the shape to the established lines—the same process as was done for the miniature. Again, use any method or tool you like to remove the wood.

After the basic shape is rounded by carving, it can be finished with a rasp. As you can see from the picture, the carving does not have to be extra smooth; the rasp can be used to finish and smooth the cuts.

To separate the pieces after carving, a knife can be inserted into the seam under the tail. A light tap can pop the body filler used to hold the pieces together.

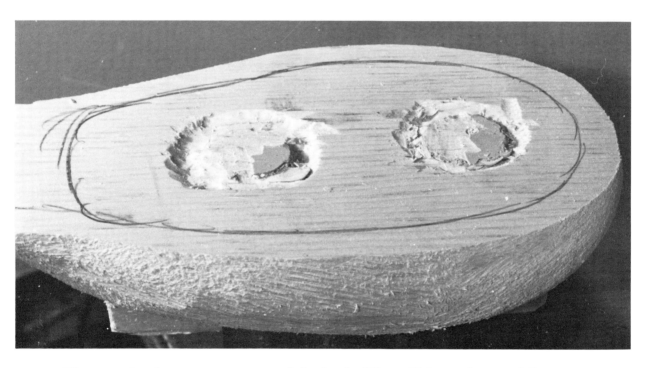

The troughs that were cut around the body filler will keep the wood from splintering any farther than the cuts. Without the troughs, it might splinter to both ends. Both sections should be marked to indicate the area to be hollowed.

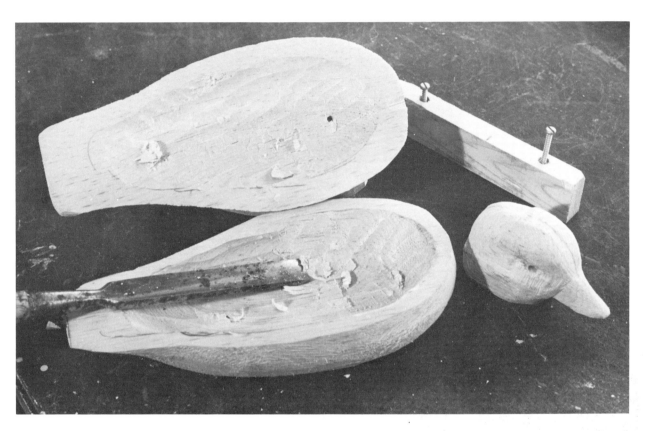

The pieces can be hollowed with a chisel or by drilling. Notice the screwhole for the head in the top piece shows due to hollowing out the top hole of the decoy. The block on the right (with screws still in it) was attached on the bottom half of the decoy and clamped into the vise.

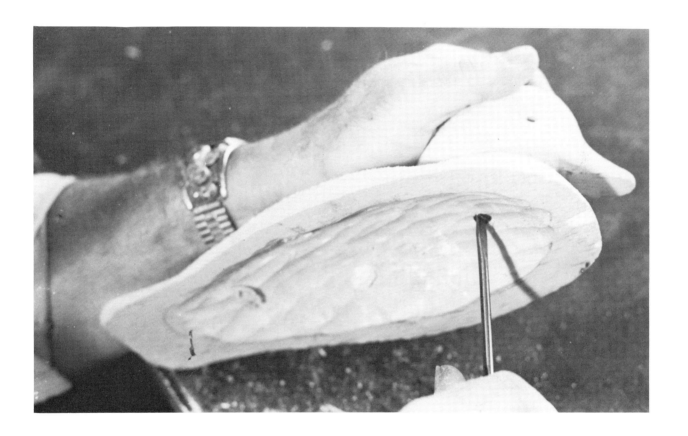

The head should be glued, then positioned as marked, and secured with a screw from the bottom.

The two sections of the body can be glued together, and the basic decoy will be complete except for finishing. An easy method of sanding is to wrap sandpaper around a paint stick and tightly staple it. (Note staples off to the left side.) Sand the entire decoy with this stick, then with pieces of hand-held sandpaper. Any imperfections will be magnified on the smooth surface, so double-check and sand again if necessary.

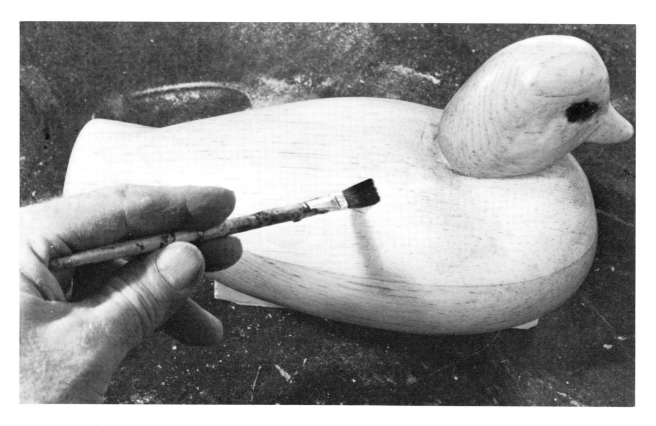

The eyes should be placed in the decoy (as shown on pages 49–54) and the decoy can then be sealed with clear wood sealer.

After the clear sealer has dried, a coat of white gesso (acrylic-based paint) can be applied to the entire decoy, including the eyes. After the decoy is dry, the pattern to be painted is marked.

The eyes can be cleaned with a knife to remove the gesso. The eyes were painted in order to seal the filler used to set the eye.

Life comes to the decoy through the eye.

The forthcoming section on painting will explain how to paint and finish your decoy. The head will be multicolored but is not justified by this black-and-white photo.

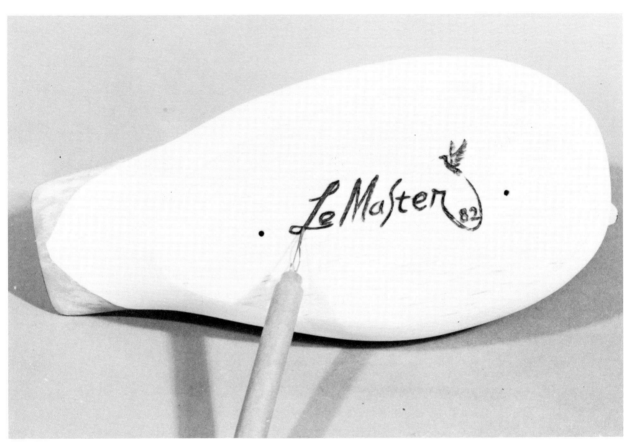

The last step is to burn or carve your signature into the bottom of the decoy. Written signatures can be destroyed in time. Assume that your decoy will be an antique someday, so let its future owners know who made it.

The Masters of Yesteryear

I live in the Illinois River Valley, which is very rich in waterfowl and decoy history. Years ago decoy carvers were to be found in every town or village along the river. Although most of their surviving decoys have been snatched by collectors, there is still an occasional find now and then. I regret that I did not start collecting decoys sooner; only after I started carving them myself did I realize their status as an art form. It also occurred to me that we are very fortunate that some of the old masters are still with us. Being able to meet and share thoughts with these people has really enriched my feelings toward the art of the decoy.

There was a time when I first started carving decoys, however, when I was very critical of the old-timers for not depicting the duck as it really appeared. I realize today how wrong I was; I didn't know the whole story then. As usual, it is much easier to be critical of others when you know only some of the facts. It didn't take me long to realize the beauty in what had been done by the masters of yesteryear. Now I find them hard to criticize as I once did.

My personal collection of decoys is not large, but what it lacks in size, it more than makes up in warmth, for I have personally known all the carvers. I regret that some of my decoy-making friends have passed on in the last decade, but each left a legacy in the art. I will always feel that I have a part of them with me because I have constant reminders of them on my shelves.

Most of the so-called old-timers started carving decoys from necessity. They could not afford to buy hunting decoys, so they learned how to make their own. There were no guidelines to follow, just the personal feelings of what each could put into his work. From making decoys for themselves, many turned to making them for others to bring in extra income.

Many old-timers stood out from the crowd. Their decoys seem to be sought most by today's collectors. All of these artists had something in common, and until I started researching I did not realize it. In their search for the design of a good hunting decoy, the carvers who gained the greatest following had perfected the key feature—they all had the head axioms right. The bodies of the various designs were secondary, but they all had the basic heads right.

Head shapes used by some masters of yesteryear.

The eyes of these decoys were properly located and the throats were positioned behind the eye. Each carver had arrived with the fundamental solution but did not know why, except that the decoy was his interpretation of the duck. It is very apparent today how observant these carvers were so many years ago. The bills did not have to be accurate, by any means, as long as they were sturdy. Some bills scooped up and some down, but the basic head conveyed all that it was meant to be. The body could be long or short, fat or thin, as long as it floated as the maker wished.

The feather designs created by most decoy makers were entirely different from each other. It is hard to believe that there could be so many different variations of feathers and colors, but rarely was there any significant similarity among carvers' decoys. Frequently, several species were carved from the same pattern. Only the painting varied to distinguish different species.

Most of the actual hunting decoys were made of cedar or pine and were hollowed to lighten them for use in the field. Some carvers immersed the whole decoy in hot linseed oil to seal the wood and make it waterproof. Oil-based paints adhered well to this base coat. The combination was very durable in the field and didn't require frequent repainting. This aspect of decoy making was true in my area but not so for the coastal decoys that were used in salt water. Salt caused the paint to deteriorate more quickly.

Decoys painted as hens usually had well-defined marks simulating the feather edges. The accuracy of the sets of feathers was of little importance as long as the basic shape and the direction in which they pointed were close.

Colors were established by painting the entire carving first, then outlining the feathers in one or two colors. A dark shaft was added to the center of each feather to give it character.

Drake decoys were easier to paint because the maker used painting combs. These combs allowed the painter to simulate the vermiculation (barlike markings on feathers). They were also used to break the harshness of large expanses of solid colors. The combs were made of a rubber that had been notched with a razor. Some were also made of metal that was slit to give it a comblike appearance. To use the comb, a light-colored undercoat was applied to the decoy. After it had dried, a darker color was painted onto the area to be vermiculated or combed. While the paint was still wet, the notched rubber (or metal) comb was zigzagged through it. This would remove the wet paint on top and expose the lighter color underneath. The comb had to be wiped clean at the end of each motion.

Some decoy carvers reversed the light and dark coats as a matter of personal preference. The effect of the combed paint was very decorative and was accomplished with little effort. Each painter had a favorite style in the use of the painting comb. Style in their carvings, combined with individualized painting styles, made these old-timers masters of their art.

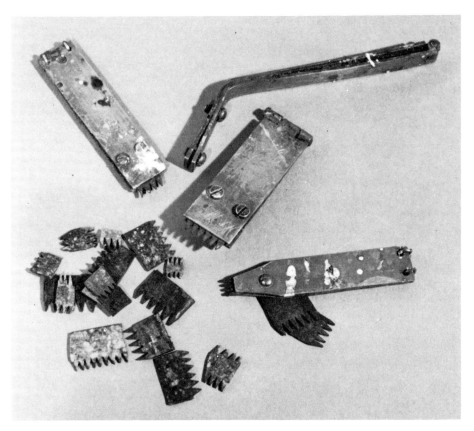

Painting combs and holders used by the late Hector Whittington.

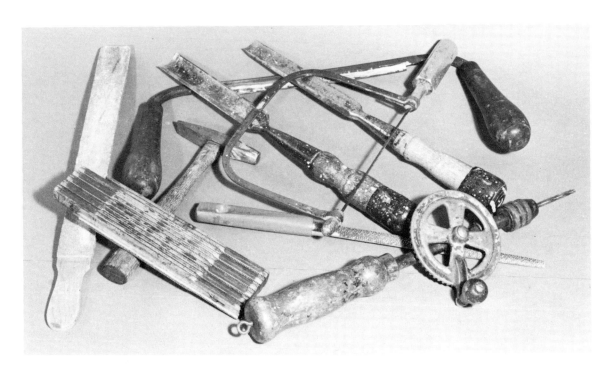

Basic tools of one of the masters.

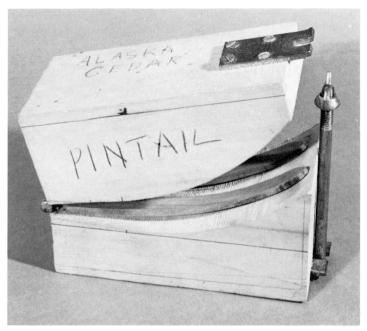

Jig used for forming hardwood tail feathers. The wood was dampened, then clamped in the jig to warp as it dried.

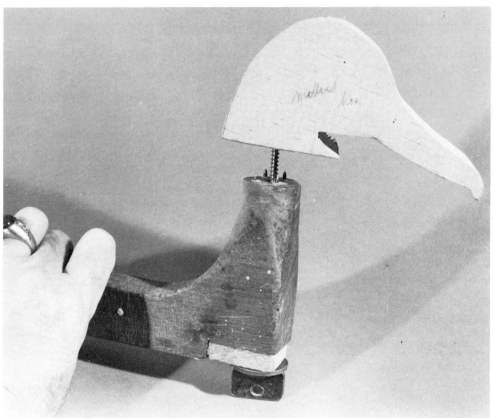

A homemade jig used to hold the head while carving. The head was tapped onto the four points, and the long screw was housed in a hole in the center of the points. The wing of the screw made it very easy to tighten the head securely, and then the jig was clamped in a vise.

Mallard hen by Lashbrook.

Two views of a Pintail hen by Lashbrook.

Two views of a Pintail hen by Whittington.

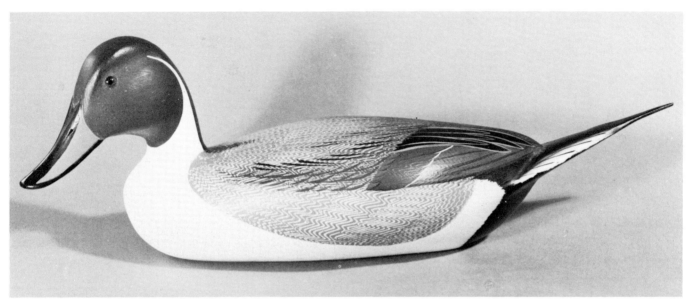

Two views of a Pintail drake by Lashbrook.

Compare each style in carving and in painting. Each artist was trying to convey his interpretation of the same species. Shape, design, and colors were all different. Even the strokes of the combing on the drakes show the personal touch. I consider all of these beautiful, without concern for their accuracy in portraying a live duck—each is a form of the art of the wooden bird.

Two views of a Pintail drake by Whittington.

Two views of a Pintail drake by Weeks.

Two views of a Pintail drake by McAlpin.

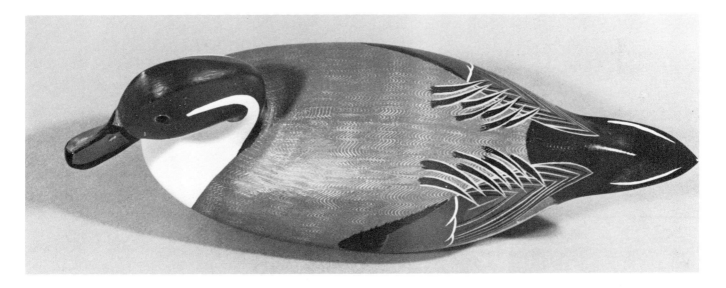

Style in Wood

A wooden decoy does not have to be painted to be pretty. Some carvers prefer a natural or stained finish for their decoys. The wood grain can lend beauty; style and grace come from the simplicity of the form. Even a knot in the wood seems to add character. The decorative-style decoy was carved from butternut wood and stained in certain areas, the ultrastylized carving was made from walnut, and the conventional decoy was sculpted from pine.

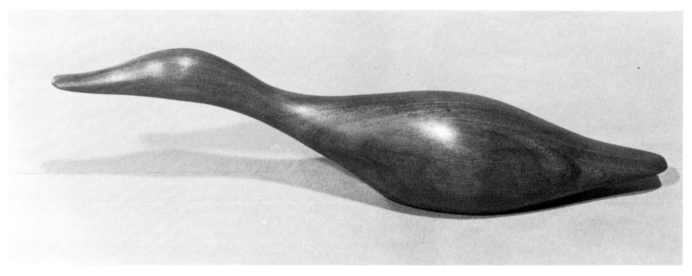

LeMaster

100

Hall

Meyer

The One-Third-Size Decoy

This lesson in carving may seem a step backwards because of the size, but is designed to help you progress in shaping the duck's anatomy without creating extra work. It will be much easier for you to complete the individual steps—*one step at a time*—on a smaller decoy and again work up to larger models.

One-Third-Size Mallard Drake Decoy

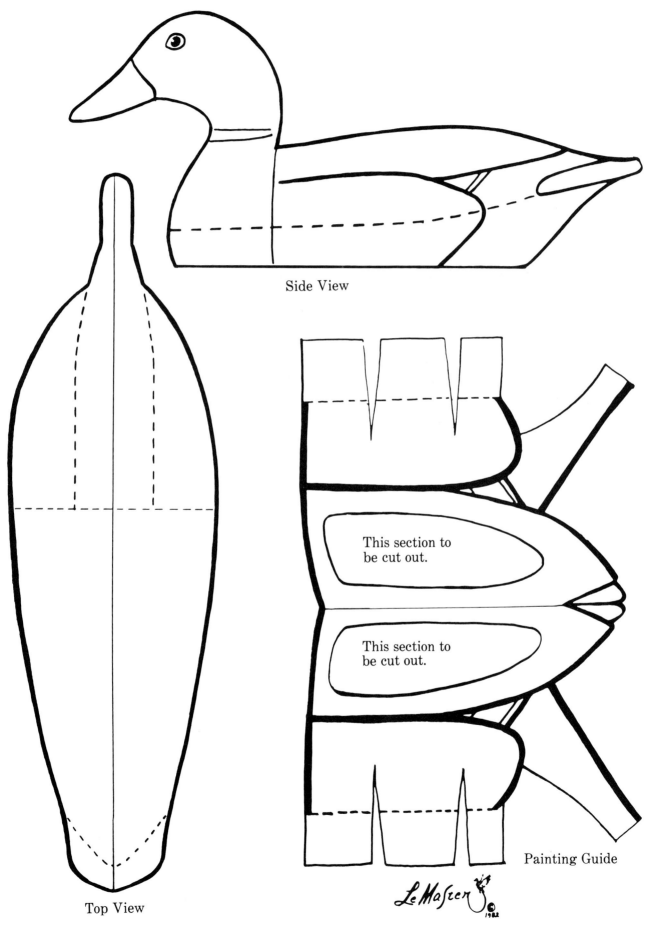

Side View

This section to
be cut out.

This section to
be cut out.

Top View

Painting Guide

The first eight steps on the one-third-size decoy are the same as for the miniature.

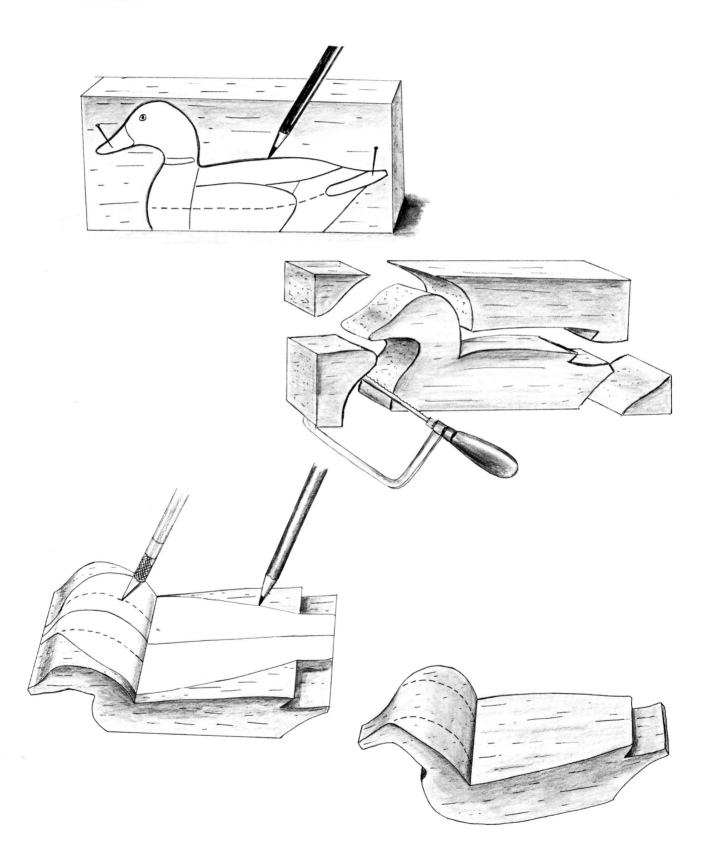

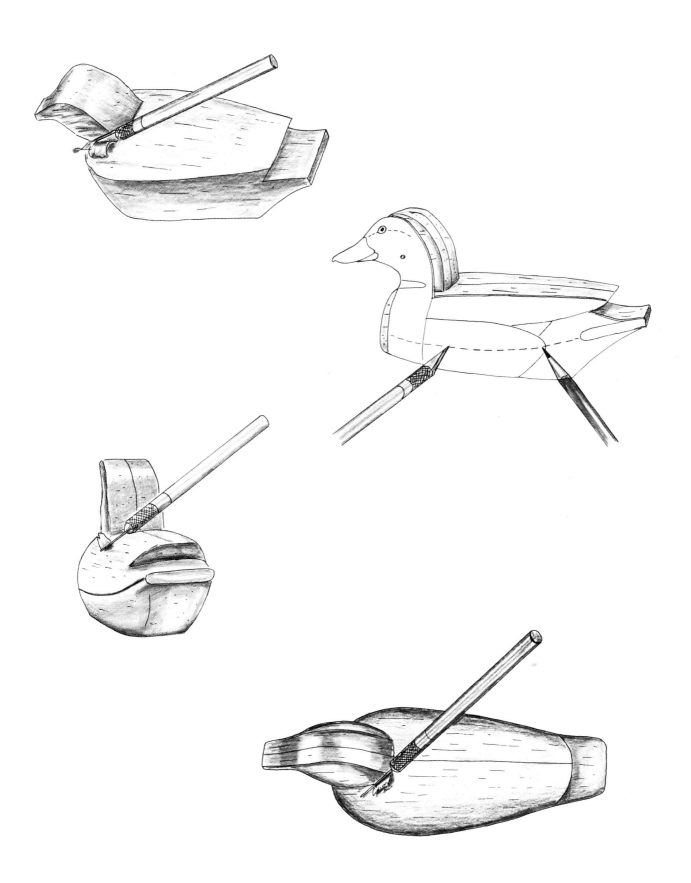

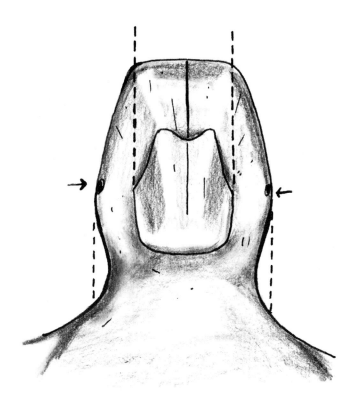

Starting with the minor refinements of the head, you can further your understanding of the real shape of the duck. The next step is to narrow the head at the top, or crown. Make sure that it is not narrower than the width of the bill where the bill joins the head, though it can be wider. At this time the hourglass shape of the neck is created by carving indentations on both sides. Do not remove any wood from the back or front of the neck, except for the corners to round the neck.

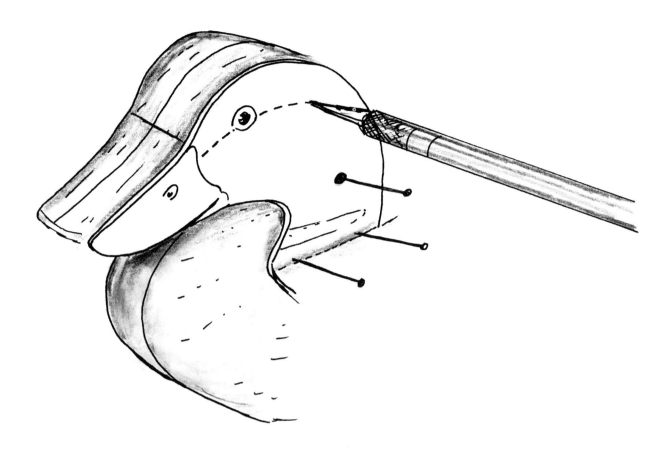

After you have rounded the head at the top and created the neck, place the pattern against the head and mark the dotted line for the eye trough (puncture with a knife or a pin). Also locate the jowl, which is indicated by the black dot on the side of the head. The eye should also be located at this time and can be drilled when the pattern is removed. If you have trouble holding the pattern on the contours, use pins to keep it in place. Do not shove them in deeply as they will create holes that may have to be filled later.

On the previous illustration a dotted line was marked to show the area of indentation in front and behind the eye called the eye trough. It is a shallow depression and has very gentle slopes. The jowl area, marked by the black dot, is the widest area of the head. The contour of the jaw tapers from that point. If you have removed the mark showing the eye placement, it can be reinstated by using the pattern again. Do not hesitate to reestablish whatever needs to be shown to keep your reference marks visible. Try to shape the bill so it is similar to that in the drawing. This is another step in learning to observe and to transfer an intricate shape to a carving.

As you progress with each step, more contours will need to be established on the carving. In order to do this, wrap the painting guide over the carving and make sure it is evenly centered. When it's in position, pin the tabs to the bottom. With the guide firmly in place, mark the sidepocket area by tracing or puncturing. This line is indicated by the thick line at the end of the pencil. Make sure that you mark both *sides before removing the guide.*

With the lines marked on each side of the decoy, the next step is to create the indentation of the sidepocket. This pocket is actually a group or set of feathers that covers the wing when folded and resting. The pocket bulges from being pushed out by the wing underneath it. Since the outside dimensions of the decoy were established by the size of the pattern, all contours are within the

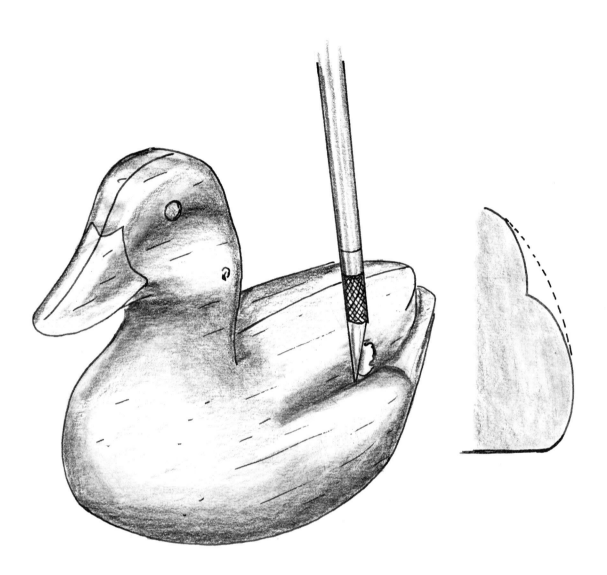

original shape's parameters. To create a bulge, the wood has to be removed so one area is higher than another. When working with wood, the puffier you want something to look, the deeper the wood must be removed along that area. The sidepocket is created by cutting in on the lines marked and angling to this cut from the top and bottom. The edges are then rounded toward the crevice created by the cut.

The body tapers to a ∨-shape under the tail. This area can be carved at this time. Always keep the roundness in mind as you make each cut.

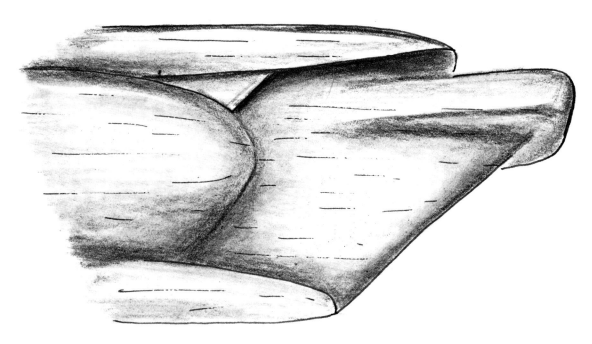

Decision time: The area shown in the first drawing can be carved or undercut as depicted. This is not necessary to the total outcome of the carving, but it will give the decoy more character.

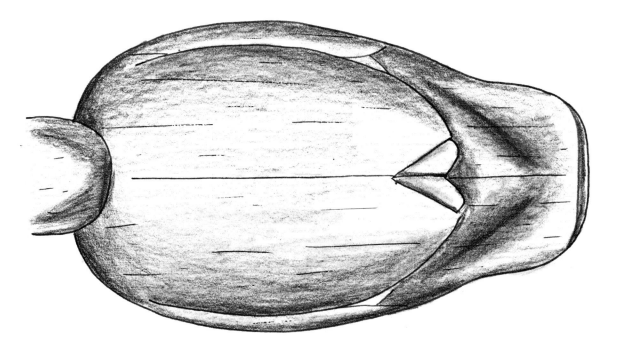

The area above the tail in the second drawing is tapered to a **V**-*shape similar to the step that was done on the underside.*

The tips of the wings can be established while you are working in this area. If you have difficulty in marking their location, you can use the guide to check the location.

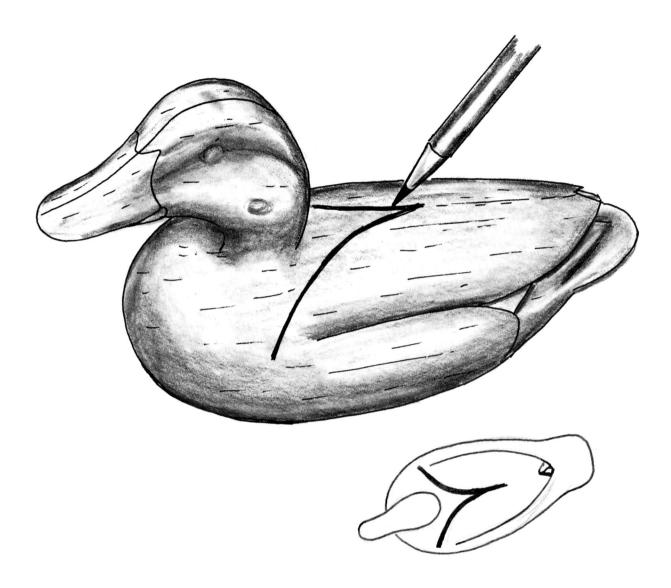

The final contour of the body is a Y*-shaped depression that starts in the middle of the back and goes down each side behind the neck, as shown. I like to think of this as the rain gutter—if it rains, the water will run down the center to the neck and then off to each side.*

The actual depression does not extend much lower than the front of the sidepocket. Mark lines on the carving so you have a guide to follow. Don't get too close to the back of the neck, as wood must be left so the neck can taper gently to the cut.

A trenchlike cut is made, following the lines as guides. The cut can be made with a chisel, a knife, or even a round file. Make sure the cut is not too deep. It is always better to take a little off at a time until satisfied with the contours. When the carving has reached this point, the last thing you want to do is ruin it because of carelessness. A little at a time *is the key.* The smaller drawing shows the gentle slopes of the finished cuts.

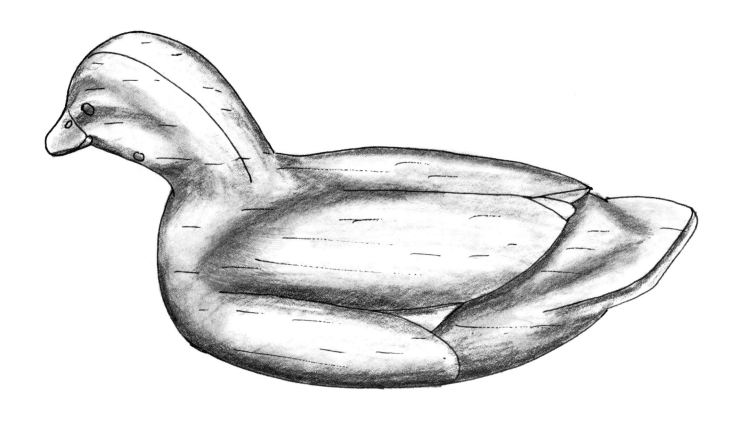

The centerline established at the beginning of the carving should still be there, except for the trough area that was cut on the last step. If you have completed the shape to your satisfaction, the knife can be put away. Now, it is time for sanding. Sand the carving until all cutting marks are removed and the surface is smooth.

When you are finished sanding and are sure that the decoy is really smooth—sand it again (you will find things you missed the first time). Then, paint the carving with white interior latex or gesso and let it dry. The eyes can be set at this time (refer to the section on eyes on pages 48–54).

You will not need a painting guide for this carving if you have followed the procedures as set forth. I included a guide in the pattern for marking the sidepocket and wings only. If you feel you need it, proceed in the same way as for the miniature.

Most of the lines are defined by the contours except for the neck ring, breast line, and tail. When you are finally ready to paint, refer to the color section between pages 124 and 125 for pointers on painting and color.

The Variables of Color

Painting—the very word or thought elicits more uncertainty than any other aspect of making decoys. Many excellent decoy carvers are reluctant to try painting their work. Often they decide that staining is the best way to finish their carvings. Why should it evoke so much uncertainty? Most carvers, when queried, usually answer, "I'm not an artist—I can carve but I can't paint." I have a simple response to that: "You do not have to be an artist to paint."

The truth is that decoy makers are intrigued by carving, and they make an effort to learn as much as they can about it. It probably started when they were young, with a pocket knife and whittling wood, a simple project with simple methods of doing it. The outcome might not have been excellent, but at least the basic challenge could be met. Painting can also be conquered—it's just a matter whether you want to devote the same effort to painting as you have devoted to carving.

When carving, you *feel* the cutting or removal of the wood. With painting, there is almost a total absence of *feel* while working. Sight is the key to painting, and your sense of touch is not really needed. With painting, you *watch* what you are doing—not *feel*. Perhaps this is what scares people. Of course, there is some application of the touching sense as you mix the paints, but it will be sight that you grow to rely on.

I have attempted to show in previous sections that anyone can carve. My goal in this section is to explain painting so it can be done one step at a time—just as in carving. To break it down, painting is nothing more than applying color to an area of your choice.

If there is criticism, it's because others see it differently and feel that you should have done it their way. Let them do it their way—you do it the way you want it. The only person in the world who has to be

118

satisfied is the person creating the work. However, we are rarely satisfied with our own work because we usually see the areas that could have been better. Change it on the next one if you like, but make sure it's your decision and not because someone thought it was wrong.

Frequently, my wife and I disagree about color. I may see a certain color as orange and she may think it's closer to red. To me, I detect some yellow in it; to her the yellow doesn't appear as strong, so she calls it red. Determining exact colors is a personal matter. People rarely see color alike. It may appear that I am making rigid statements about colors, but keep in mind that this book represents only how I go about making and painting decoys. It does not mean that everyone will, or should, agree with my views on color. Using color involves personal decisions.

How can you tell which color is right? That's a tough one because there are so many variables. We'll concern ourselves only with ducks, since this is our objective.

Many excellent full-color photographs of ducks have been printed in magazines and books. With time and perseverance, you can gather quite a collection of photos to help you with some color decisions. Most of the photographs will be acceptably accurate. That is, the colors may vary a little but by no wider a margin than they do in actual life. Colors do vary from duck to duck.

Mallard drakes are supposed to have an iridescent green head, yet I have seen some with the prettiest blue iridescence you have ever seen. It is common for the Mallard drake to have some blue or violet on the rear of its head, but these ducks had blue over the entire head and no green at all. What would happen if this were the first one you were able to get your hands on to study? Would you be wrong in using blue? You certainly would be challenged by most duck enthusiasts if you painted a Mallard with a blue head.

If you want to be sure—there is safety in numbers, as the old saying goes. Look at as many ducks as you can and try to notice the variations. I have a painting at home of a Mallard hen in which the artist depicts a very distinctive white ring around the neck. Everyone knows that the Mallard drake has the ring around the neck and not the hen. Should I challenge the authenticity of it? I would probably be the first in a long line to say so if not for the fact that I have seen not only one live hen with the neckring, but several. I was told by a professional biologist that one in every 1,000 Mallards has enough genes of the opposite sex to show visual traits of both sexes. I have seen several paintings that portrayed Mallard hens this way. But when they show teal feathers on the sidepocket of the Mallard hen, it's time to challenge the artist's sources. If you are wondering what all of this has to do with painting, I am demonstrating that there is latitude and freedom for personal choices in choosing colors as long as you have done your homework.

Back to color: Pictures can really be a help, but they can also be a hindrance. Only experience will determine where the line should be drawn for you. Before you decide that a single picture is good enough, let me relate an experience. Several years ago I was having some colored photographs processed for *Wildlife in Wood*. While visiting with one of the lab employees, I was told of one of their dissatisfied customers. It seems that the customer had taken Christmas pictures and wanted an enlargement of his Christmas tree. Using his negative, they developed the picture, though with some difficulty. The real difficulty came, however, when the customer picked up the picture. He had taken a picture of his pink-flocked Christmas tree and the lab people had turned it green in the final photograph. Colors can be changed in the lab and with printing, perhaps not that drastic most of the time but it is something to be aware of when justifying color choices to a single photo.

The references used most often for color are mounts or skins. Next to the live duck, these are the closest you can get to the true colors. Certain problems can also arise with their use but they are not as significant. When the duck is alive, the feathers are convex both from the front to the rear, from side to side, with airspace under each one. Each feather is translucent with light penetrating and reflecting from the roundness of the underlying feathers. The colors are vivid due to the prismatic effect of bouncing light. When the duck dies and rigor mortis sets in, the muscles contract and the feathers flatten. As the feathers compress, the colors dull and lose the vibrancy of life. If the duck has exceptional plumage and the hunter wishes to mount it, it should be placed in the deep freeze until it can be processed.

If I leave a brush on its bristles overnight, I usually end up with a ruined brush. The bristles take a set and rarely can be returned to their original shape. Feathers are much the same way: Once they take a set, they can rarely be brought back to their original shape. Freezing for a length of time will make the feathers take a set the same as a brush will do in a container. The taxidermist can shampoo and clean, dry and fluff, select and arrange the feathers, but cannot give them the color they had in life. This is not meant to belittle the taxidermists; it is one of many problems they have to overcome. I would suggest that you research your subject thoroughly before you use a mounted specimen as the true shape to copy. Even mounts in museums are rarely good examples of the actual shapes of live ducks.

Use extreme caution when copying an artist's rendering—both in shape and in color. If the artist made a mistake, all you will do is pass it on. Research and reference are just as important for the colors and painting as for the body shape and carving.

Paints

There are a lot of pros and cons on selecting one type of paint over another. Let me explain the basics of the three main types of paint available.

Oils

Oil-based paints have stood the test of time. From the old masters to contemporary artists, oil paints have been used extensively. Oil paint exudes brilliance and luster. The color pigment is mixed in an oil base, and the paint is fairly thick as it comes from the tube. If you are painting on canvas, the paint can be applied with a palette knife or a brush. When using a brush on decoys, the paint should be thinned with turpentine or mineral spirits, if you want to thin the paint. Oil paints can be worked very slowly since they are very slow to dry (days to weeks). If you care to use them, agents can be used to accelerate or speed the drying time. Most instructors believe that you should shy away from using these driers, because they can cause the paint to become brittle and, eventually, to crack. This brittle quality might damage a canvas painting since canvas is an unsteady surface, but is nothing to worry about on wooden decoys. I have used drying agents in oils and have had excellent results, in terms of speedy drying and absence of cracking.

Most art stores carry several brands of oil paints and have a wide selection of colors to choose from. Cleanup has to be done with turpentine or mineral spirits; water will not work.

Oil paints have an odor even if you use odorless thinners. This smell may be offensive to some, especially in an enclosed area. I personally love the smell of an art studio in which the artist is using oils. I can't begin to describe the feeling that entering a room filled with the smell of oil paints gives me. It seems to call out for me to don an apron, grab the palette, and splash the paint. To me, it certainly is inspiring.

One problem that prevents me from using oils on decoys is that, since I hold my carvings in my hand as I paint, it really smears. Normally oils are more expensive per tube than acrylics but stretch much farther.

Alkyds

Alkyds are a relatively new type of oil-based paint; they are much faster drying and they blend beautifully. Normal drying time is less than one day, according to manufacturers. If you are considering an oil base for painting, the alkyds are an ideal solution for beginners. They should be thinned with a medium to make them more fluid. If you mount or screw a holder of some sort to the bottom of your carving, you will not have to handle the carving before the paint dries. The working time (before it dries) is excellent for the beginner. A tube of oil or alkyd paint goes a long way, so you do not need to buy large tubes of paint for your first experiments.

Acrylics

The modern painting medium is acrylic paint. If you have never used acrylics and wonder what they are like, I suppose they could be compared to latex house paint. They are easily applied, provide excellent adhesion and clean up easily with water. Acrylics are odorless.

The same colored pigments are used in both oils and acrylics. The difference is in the vehicle (fluid) with which the color is mixed. Acrylics are a mixture of powdered pigment and liquid plastic. They dry fast—maybe too fast for some people—and do not yellow with age, while oils may. Adhesion, which is excellent except on an oily or waxy surface, comes from some degree of bulk. Thinned greatly with water, adhesion is minimal until there is a buildup of material.

Acrylics cannot be painted over oils, but oils can be used over acrylics. This layering can be an interesting way to blend colors—which is difficult sometimes with acrylics alone. Acrylics have to be dry before applying oils or alkyds; experimenting is the only way to learn this technique.

My recommendation is that you start with acrylics, since they offer the most versatility in the long run.

Beginner's Buying Guide

Paint
1 tube each:
    Red (medium)
    Yellow (medium)
    Blue (medium to deep)
    Hookers green
    Burnt umber
    Raw sienna
    White
    Ivory black
    Mars black
1 small tube of gesso

Brushes
1 each:
    ½ inch flat (synthetic)
    No. 5 or 6 round (synthetic)
    No. 2 round (synthetic)

Accessories
    Paper palette
    Paper towels
    Cup for water
    Illustration board (for color charts)

This list of supplies is as basic as I can suggest. More colors and brushes can be added later as you gain experience in painting. It will not be as inexpensive as I would like, but considering the number of decoys it will paint, it's a bargain.

If you purchase acrylic paints, make sure that they are all labeled as acrylics and not water colors. Acrylics are completely waterproof when dry; water colors are not.

Brushes with man-made fibers are acceptable—especially to start with. Normally they are less expensive and will withstand the rough treatment of someone first learning how to paint.

Paint is mixed on, and used from, a palette. The most useful palette comes in a tablet form that has disposable sheets. Some painters use a piece of glass. Plastic will not work well, for acrylic paint will stick to it after it has been scraped a few times. A piece of wax paper will work fine, especially if the edges are taped to a piece of cardboard. Anything can be used as a palette for acrylic paints, provided it is waterproof.

Two of the more popular brands of acrylics. The tip on the tube to the right is the one used to measure paints.

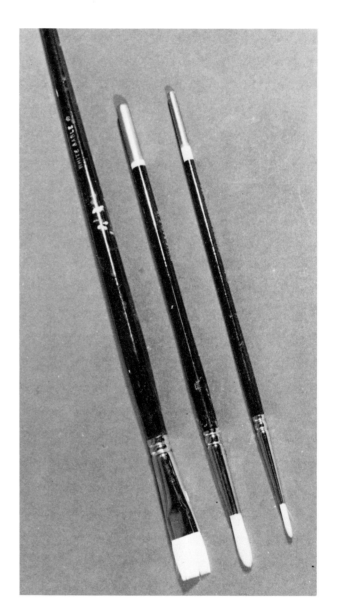

My recommendation as a starter's set of brushes.

FEATHER PATTERNS

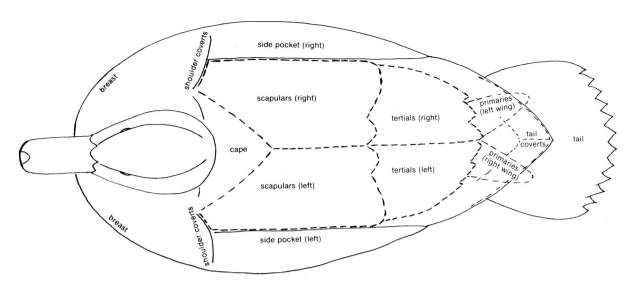

Sets of feathers.

Basic feather pattern.

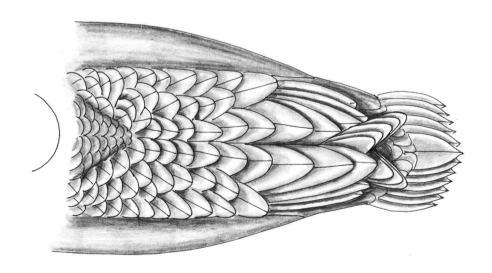

Decorative feather pattern (top view).

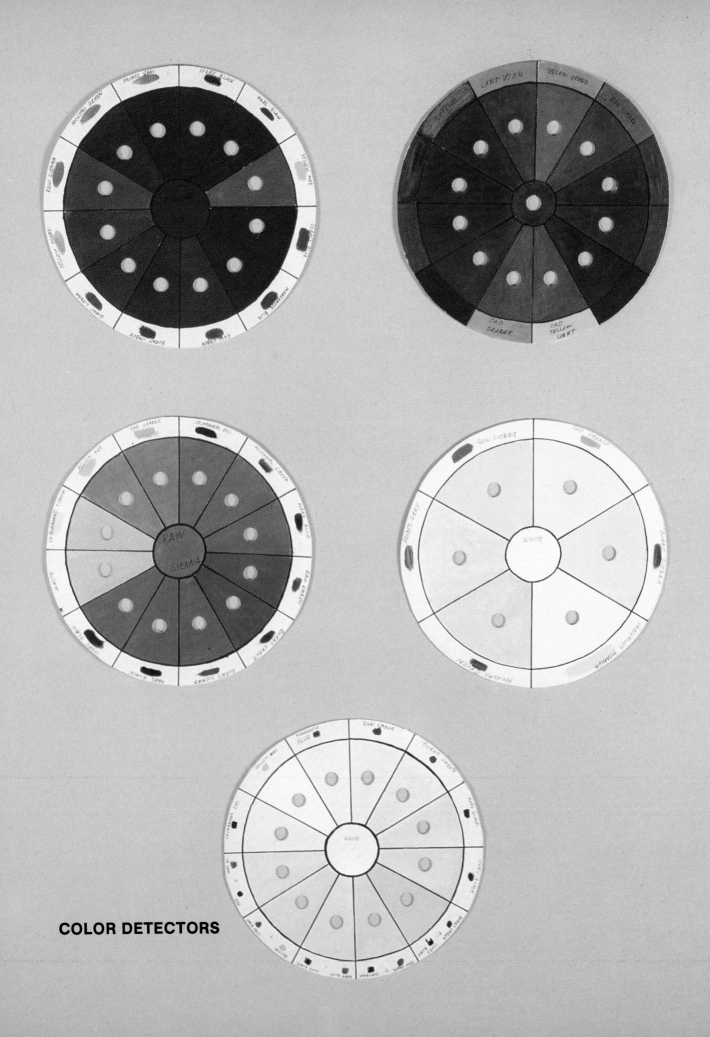

COLOR DETECTORS

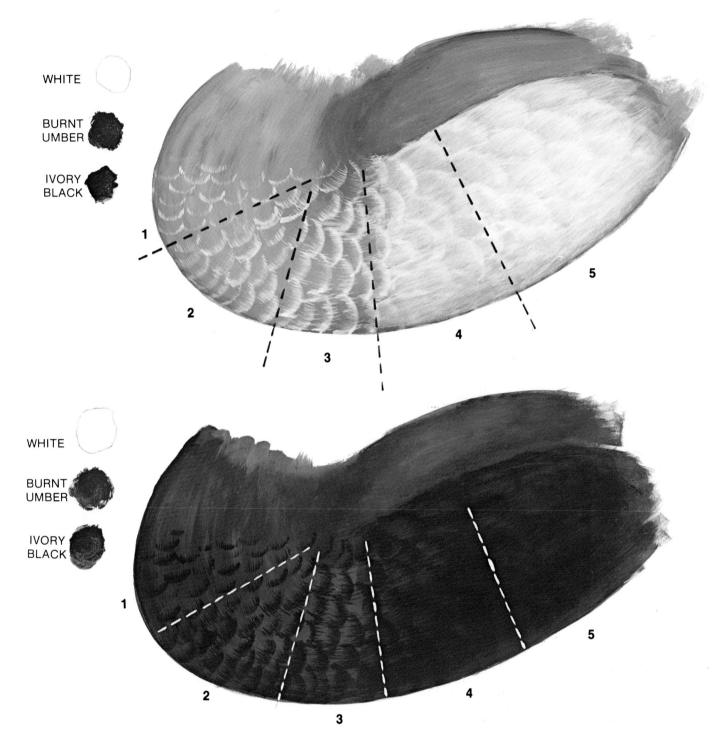

WHITE

BURNT UMBER

IVORY BLACK

1

2

3

4

5

WHITE

BURNT UMBER

IVORY BLACK

1

2

3

4

5

LIGHT ON LIGHT   DARK ON DARK

Base Color—Mixture of White-Burnt Umber-Ivory Black

1. Outline Feathers—<u>White (for light)</u>/<u>Black (for dark)</u>
2. Outline Feathers Second Time—Lengthen Strokes

3. Strengthen Feathers Third Time—Bold Breakup Strokes (Random)
4. Thinned Paint Over Entire Area Being Painted
5. Strengthen Edges of Feathers Again
Repeat last two steps if necessary

STEPS IN PAINTING MALLARD HEN

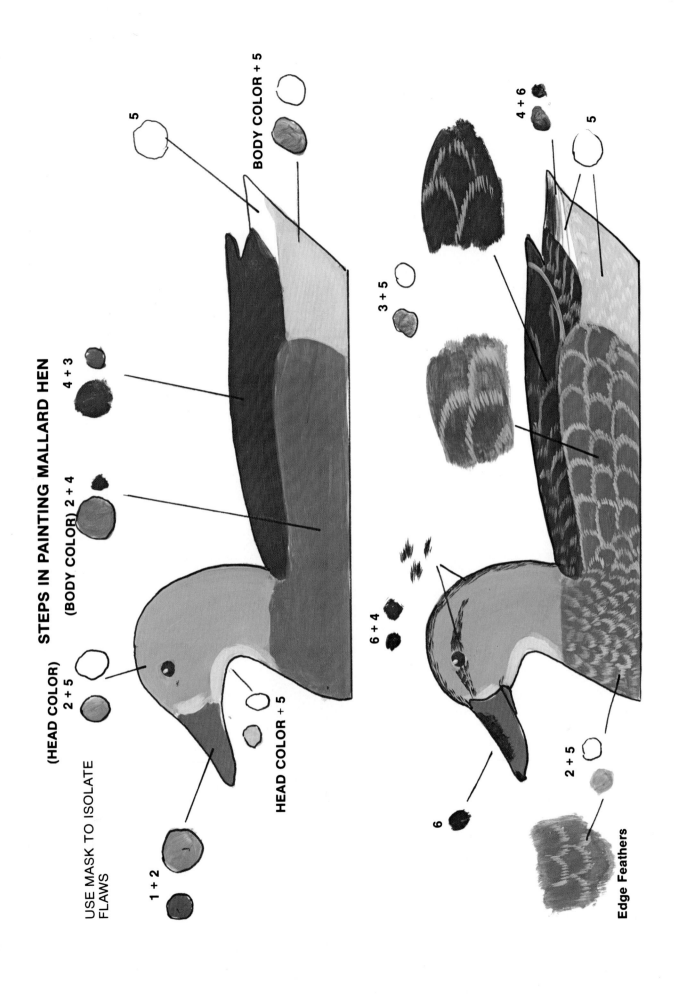

USE MASK TO ISOLATE
FLAWS

(HEAD COLOR)
2 + 5

1 + 2

(BODY COLOR) 2 + 4

4 + 3

5

BODY COLOR + 5

HEAD COLOR + 5

3 + 5

4 + 6

5

6 + 4

6

2 + 5

Edge Feathers

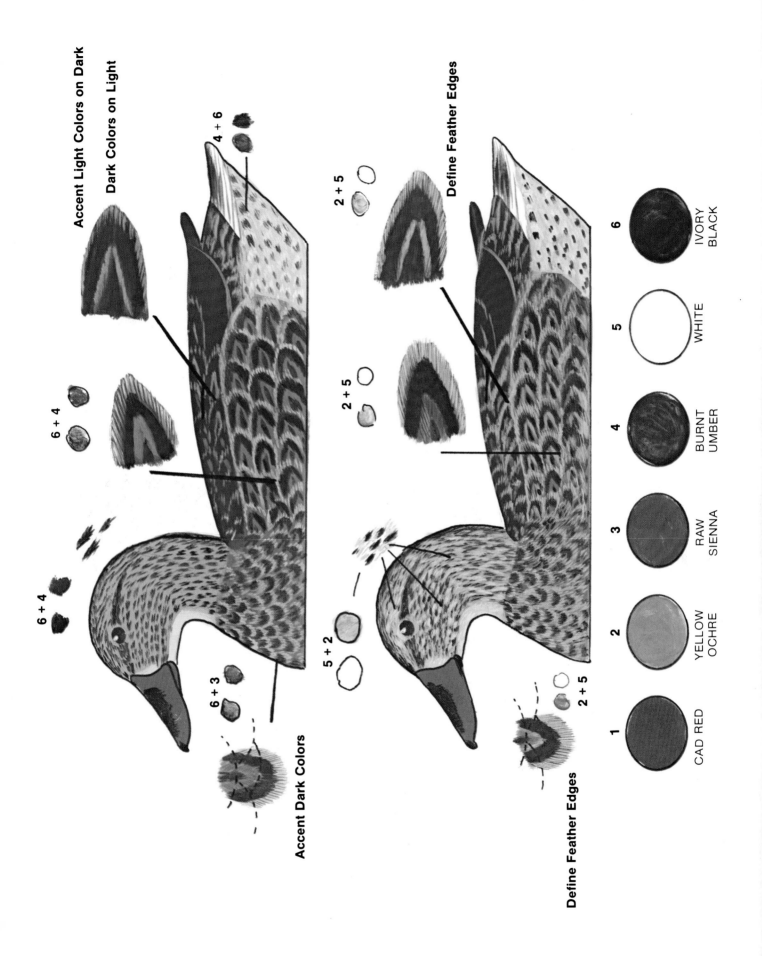

Accent Light Colors on Dark

Dark Colors on Light

4 + 6

6 + 4

6 + 4

6 + 3

Accent Dark Colors

Define Feather Edges

2 + 5

2 + 5

5 + 2

Define Feather Edges

2 + 5

Define Feather Edges

1	2	3	4	5	6
CAD RED	YELLOW OCHRE	RAW SIENNA	BURNT UMBER	WHITE	IVORY BLACK

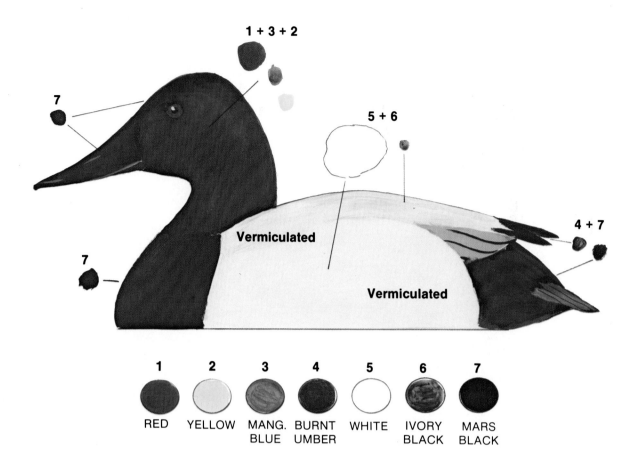

1 + 3 + 2

7

5 + 6

4 + 7

7

Vermiculated

Vermiculated

1	2	3	4	5	6	7
RED	YELLOW	MANG. BLUE	BURNT UMBER	WHITE	IVORY BLACK	MARS BLACK

CANVASBACK (DRAKE)

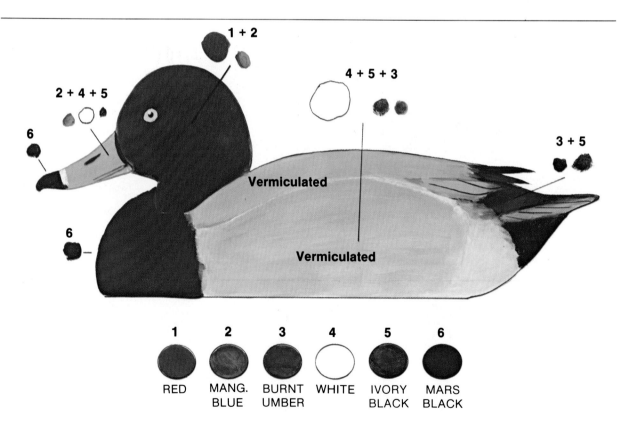

1 + 2

2 + 4 + 5

6

4 + 5 + 3

3 + 5

6

Vermiculated

Vermiculated

1	2	3	4	5	6
RED	MANG. BLUE	BURNT UMBER	WHITE	IVORY BLACK	MARS BLACK

REDHEAD (DRAKE)

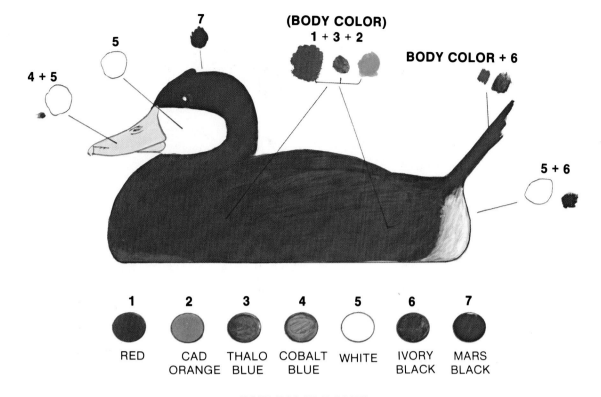

1	2	3	4	5	6	7
RED	CAD ORANGE	THALO BLUE	COBALT BLUE	WHITE	IVORY BLACK	MARS BLACK

RUDDY (DRAKE)

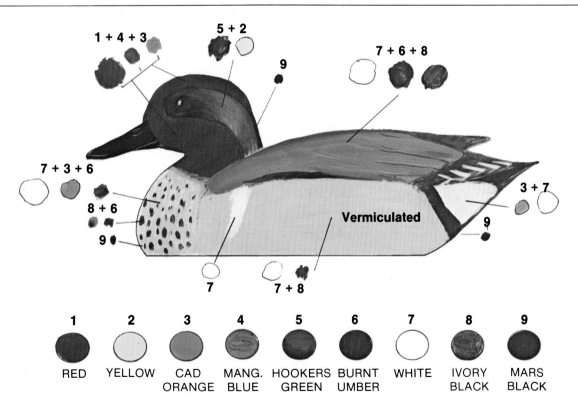

1	2	3	4	5	6	7	8	9
RED	YELLOW	CAD ORANGE	MANG. BLUE	HOOKERS GREEN	BURNT UMBER	WHITE	IVORY BLACK	MARS BLACK

GREEN-WINGED TEAL (DRAKE)

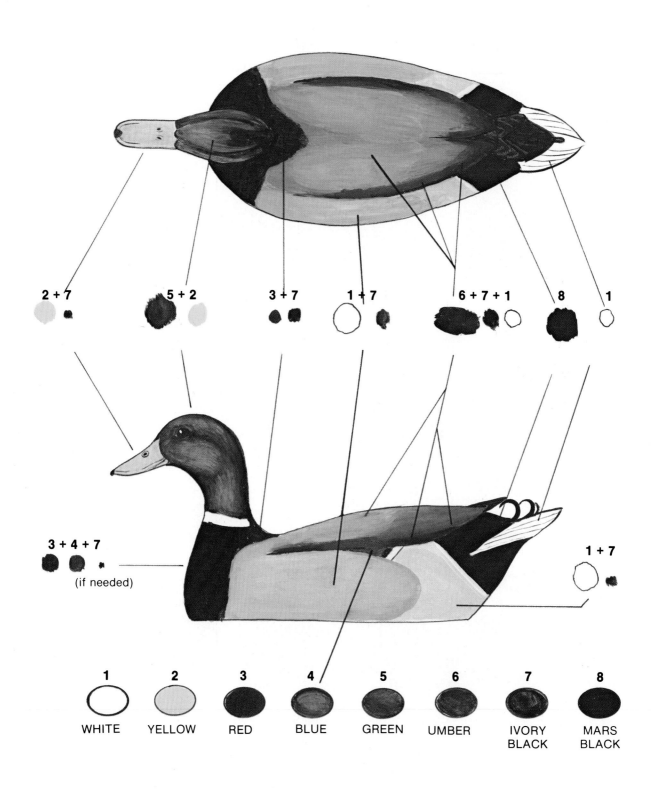

2 + 7

5 + 2

3 + 7

1 + 7

6 + 7 + 1

8

1

3 + 4 + 7

(if needed)

1 + 7

1	2	3	4	5	6	7	8
WHITE	YELLOW	RED	BLUE	GREEN	UMBER	IVORY BLACK	MARS BLACK

MALLARD (DRAKE)

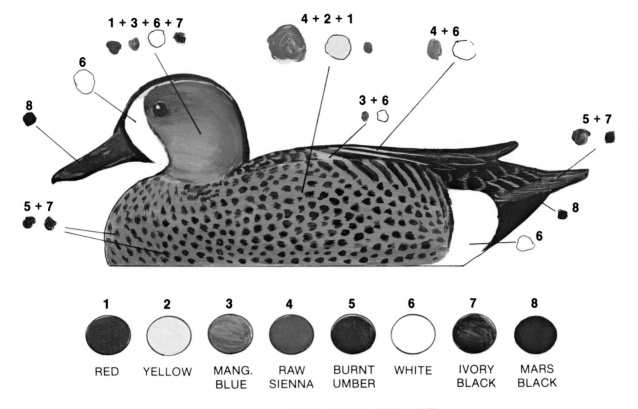

BLUE-WINGED TEAL (DRAKE)

1	2	3	4	5	6	7	8
RED	YELLOW	MANG. BLUE	RAW SIENNA	BURNT UMBER	WHITE	IVORY BLACK	MARS BLACK

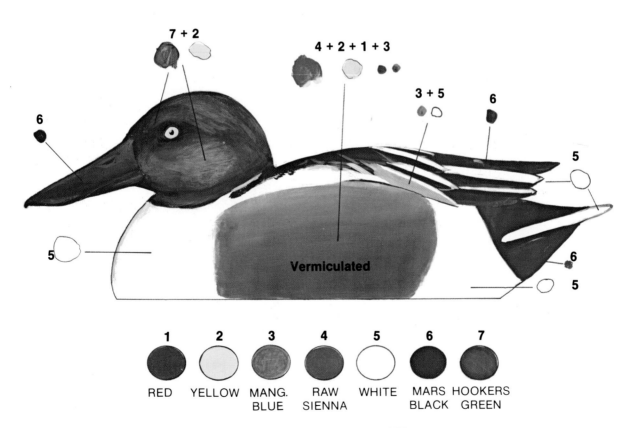

SHOVELER (DRAKE)

1	2	3	4	5	6	7
RED	YELLOW	MANG. BLUE	RAW SIENNA	WHITE	MARS BLACK	HOOKERS GREEN

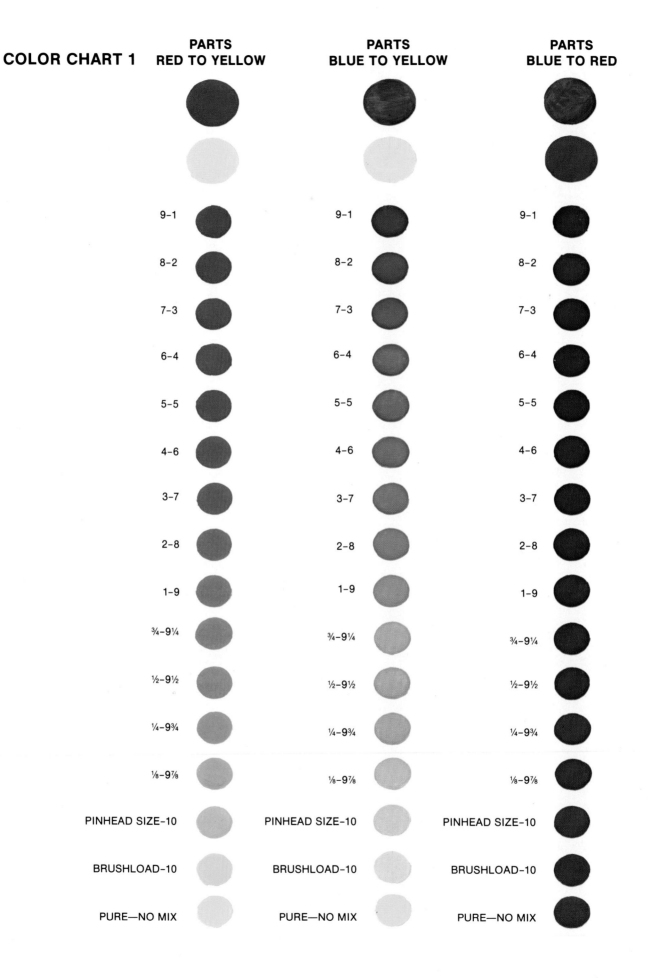

COLOR CHART 1

PARTS RED TO YELLOW	PARTS BLUE TO YELLOW	PARTS BLUE TO RED
9–1	9–1	9–1
8–2	8–2	8–2
7–3	7–3	7–3
6–4	6–4	6–4
5–5	5–5	5–5
4–6	4–6	4–6
3–7	3–7	3–7
2–8	2–8	2–8
1–9	1–9	1–9
¾–9¼	¾–9¼	¾–9¼
½–9½	½–9½	½–9½
¼–9¾	¼–9¾	¼–9¾
⅛–9⅞	⅛–9⅞	⅛–9⅞
PINHEAD SIZE–10	PINHEAD SIZE–10	PINHEAD SIZE–10
BRUSHLOAD–10	BRUSHLOAD–10	BRUSHLOAD–10
PURE—NO MIX	PURE—NO MIX	PURE—NO MIX

COLOR CHART 2

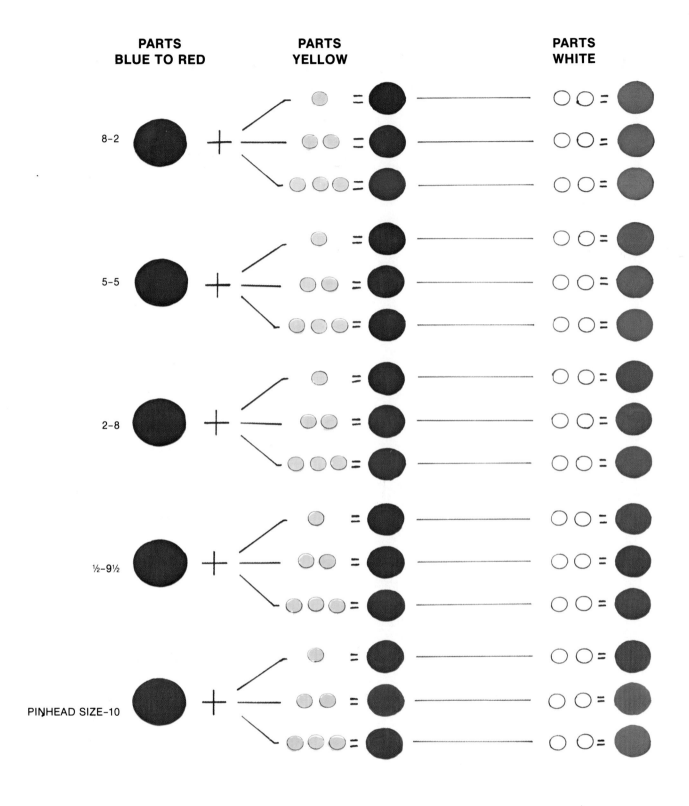

COLOR CHART 3

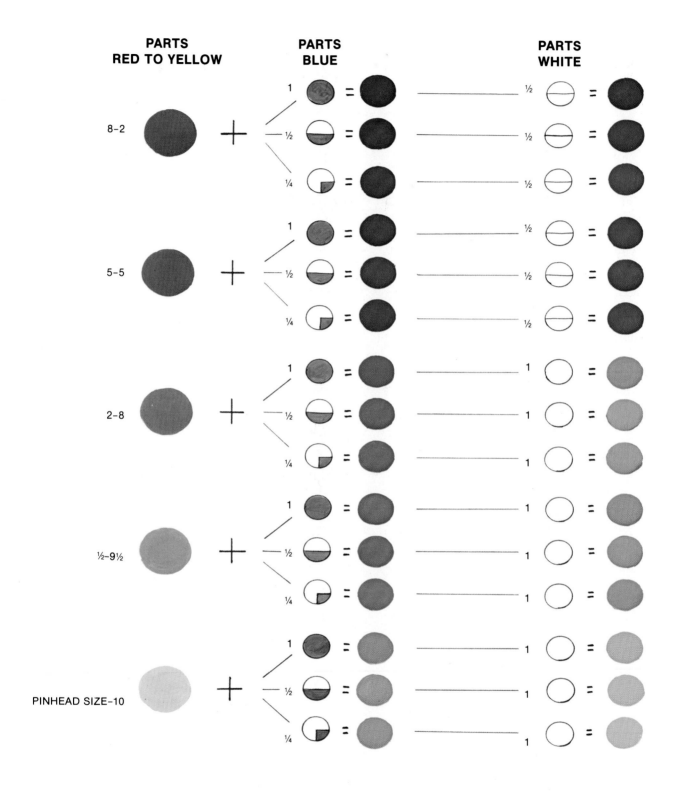

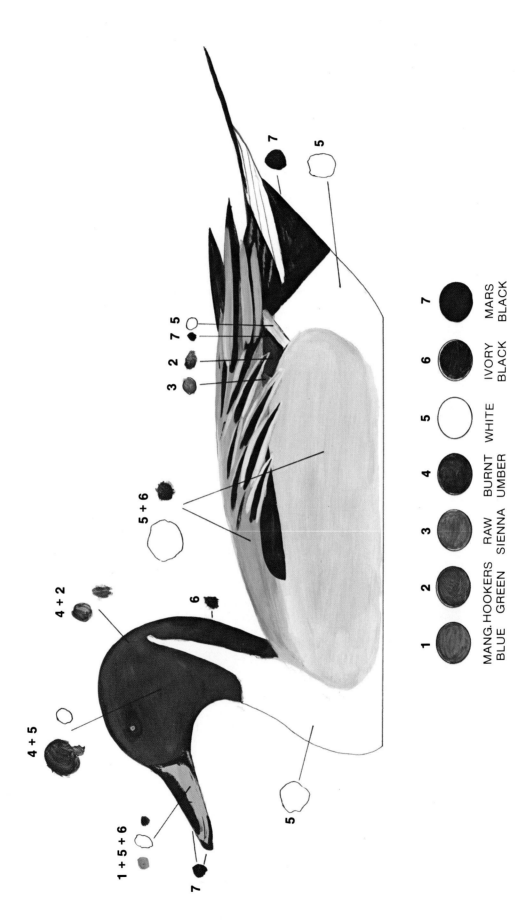

PINTAIL (DRAKE)

1	2	3	4	5	6	7
MANG. BLUE	HOOKERS GREEN	RAW SIENNA	BURNT UMBER	WHITE	IVORY BLACK	MARS BLACK

7

5

3 2 7 5

5 + 6

4 + 2

4 + 5

1 + 5 + 6

6

7

5

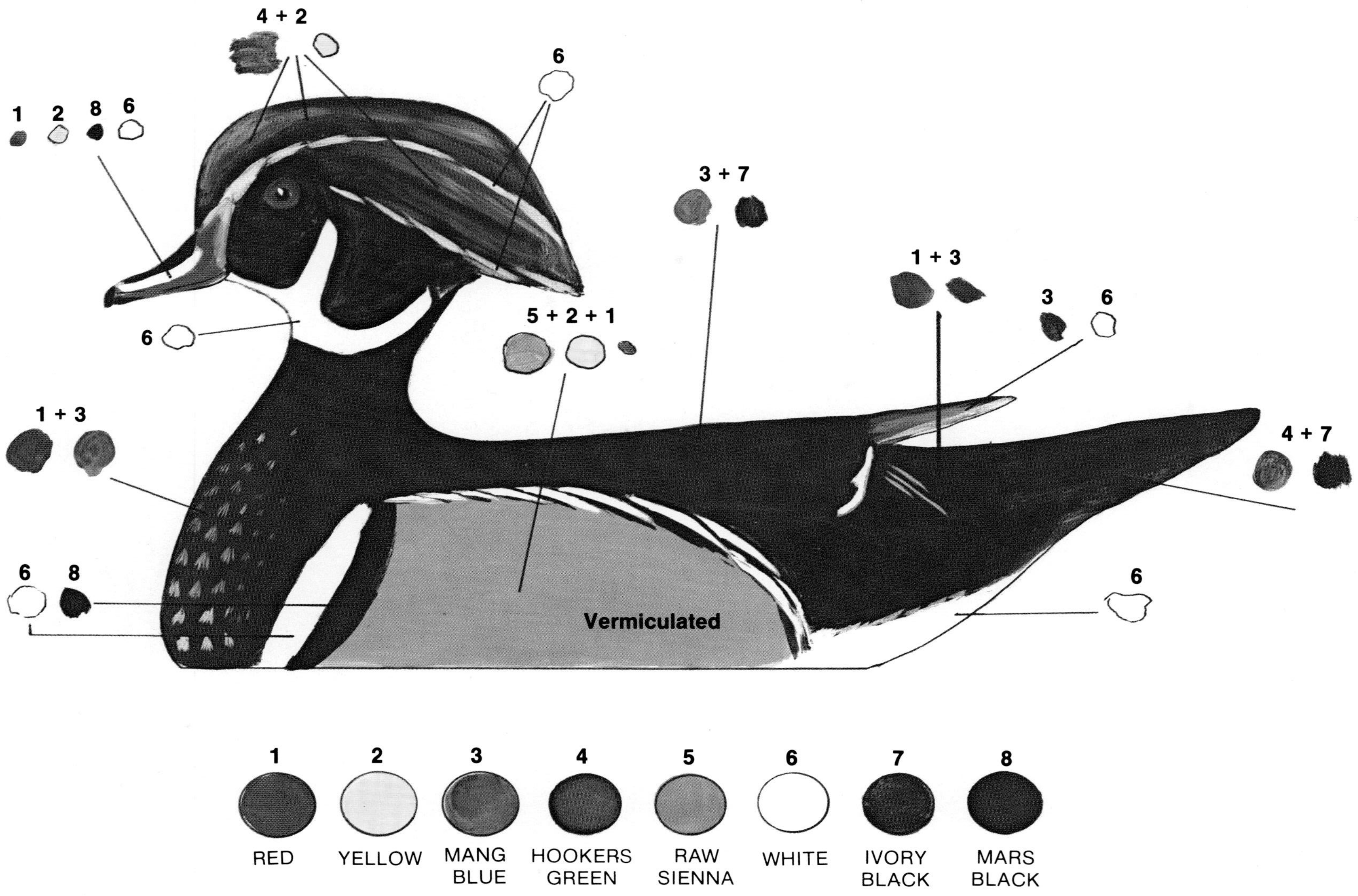

WOOD DUCK (DRAKE)

Vermiculated

4 + 7

6

3 + 7

1 + 3

3   6

5 + 2 + 1

6

4 + 2

1 2 8 6

6

1 + 3

6 8

1	2	3	4	5	6	7	8
RED	YELLOW	MANG BLUE	HOOKERS GREEN	RAW SIENNA	WHITE	IVORY BLACK	MARS BLACK

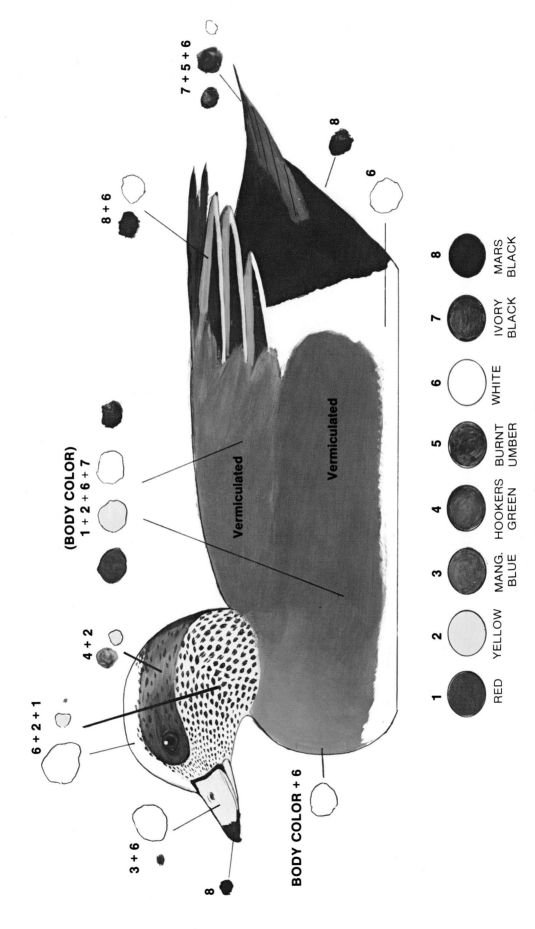

7 + 5 + 6

8 + 6

8

6

(BODY COLOR)
1 + 2 + 6 + 7

4 + 2

Vermiculated

Vermiculated

6 + 2 + 1

3 + 6

8

BODY COLOR + 6

1	2	3	4	5	6	7	8
RED	YELLOW	MANG. BLUE	HOOKERS GREEN	BURNT UMBER	WHITE	IVORY BLACK	MARS BLACK

WIGEON (DRAKE)

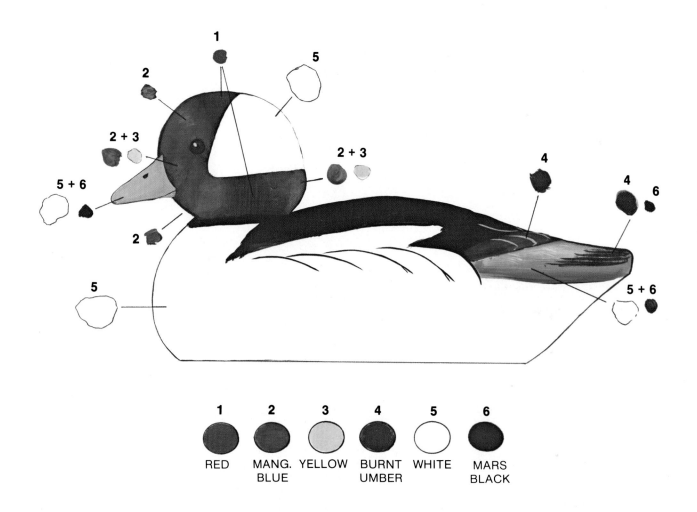

1 **2** **3** **4** **5** **6**

RED | MANG. BLUE | YELLOW | BURNT UMBER | WHITE | MARS BLACK

BUFFLEHEAD (DRAKE)

The Confusion of Color

One of my first thoughts while writing this book was to gather various manufacturers' information on paint. It was my idea to pass along the color information that the paint companies issue. I made a trip to several art stores and brought home a pile of information that would have satisfied the most inquisitive. When I finished wading through the material, though, I was really confused. It was mind-boggling to say the least. The literature seemed to be written by chemical engineers with advanced degrees who were trying to pass the information on to others of similar backgrounds.

Terms like *spectrum, primaries, secondaries, complimentary, triadic, values, hues, chroma, intensity* were meaningless to me—all I wanted was to paint a decoy. The colors have already been chosen for me, all I wanted to know was how to mix them.

Ask how to mix those colors at the local art store and, most likely, you will be shown a color wheel. It will show lots of colors, but rarely any of the ones you would use to realistically paint a duck. The art store people may show how to mix any two of the primary colors, but usually don't show what happens when the third primary color is also mixed in.

So, to avoid confusion, let me explain that the primary colors are red, yellow, and blue. All other colors will come from mixing these colors. Adding black or white will darken or lighten the colors. If three colors can be mixed and make any color, why did I have you buy so many tubes of paint? There are many shades of red, yellow, and blue. And sometimes it takes a mixture of different shades to reach a desired color. By the time you buy all possible shades, you would have spent a bundle. I guarantee that any decoy I have ever seen can be painted using the paints on my list.

The colors of nature's subjects are frequently a result of mixing all three of the primary colors with gradations of black or white. I do not mean that equal parts of each are blended, but that various amounts of each can create the desired color.

Several man-made problems will have to be overcome. Paint is a mixture of powdered color and a carrier or vehicle, as I mentioned earlier. The color is made by superfine grinding of compounds or natural substances. Sometimes there is a difference from one batch to another at the manufacturer, so the color will vary with each mixing. They try to maintain a tight line on this, but are not always successful. Another problem is caused by different manufacturers producing varied colors, even though they are labeled the same. This can be in your favor if you can detect the variances. Each manufacturer has its own name for certain colors it considers distinctive. The amount of pigment (actual color), which determines whether one coat will be enough, also varies. You can discover advantages to each of these problems by learning about the characteristics of each brand of paint. Your solution is to obtain personal experience with each.

No matter how much information I provide in this book, however, it is still up to you to *jump in* and move the paint around until you are comfortable with the outcome. Nothing and no one can do it for you. There are no secrets to painting—just work.

Remember, take it one step at a time.

I previously mentioned a color wheel. In all honesty though, the manufactured color wheel is not going to help you much with the colors you need for decoys. Your salvation lies in doing it yourself.

During my years of building models for industry, the one thing that became self-evident was the fact that if it got done, I had to do it. No one was there to do it for me and rarely was there anyone to turn to for help. Self-confidence will take you all the way—I'll do my part in breaking things down for you, but you still have to be the one doing it.

The Color Detector

How do I know which colors to mix? That question is asked more frequently than all others about painting put together. I was faced with conveying an answer to this at one of my painting seminars. I thought over and over about the problems each person has in determining a color and how we all see things differently. After some thought, I was able to devise a do-it-yourself project to solve the problem—the color detector. It is very simple and will help you, but its effectiveness will depend on your determination to learn about color. After all, the more often you do something, even mixing paint, the more comfortable and easier it becomes.

My color detector is a simplified color wheel. The basic difference between them—besides the colors—is that there are holes cut in the middle of the samples so you can have color surrounding the color you wish to detect. The untrained eye can easily be fooled by putting color chips next to another color. One color needs to be surrounded by the other before you can really see differences. All colors on the detector are tube colors (i.e., direct from the tube without mixing). The center colors can be any shade or color you wish as long as it is a purchased color and not self-mixed. I would strongly suggest that the center color should be brown if you want to compare brown tones, blue if you want blue tones, green for green tones, and so on.

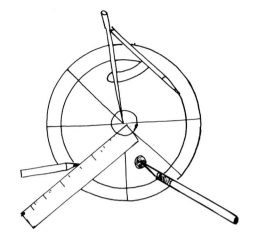

Color detector can be made with compass, straight edge, and knife. Cut holes in each section as marked.

Apply base color in the center of the circle. Mixtures of it with other colors should be painted in sections around holes.

The colors on the outside edge of the wheel should consist of the primary colors, red, yellow, and blue, then browns, ivory black, green, and any other color you might like to experiment with. You can also use other shades of the same color if you wish. The important factor is that all *colors should come directly from manufactured paint and not mixed yourself—at least for the time being. Once you establish what colors you would like to mix, it is important that you can readily obtain these colors and not have to depend initially on your skills to intermix the paint.*

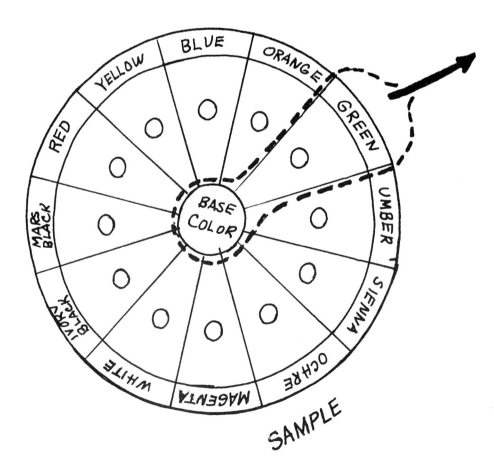

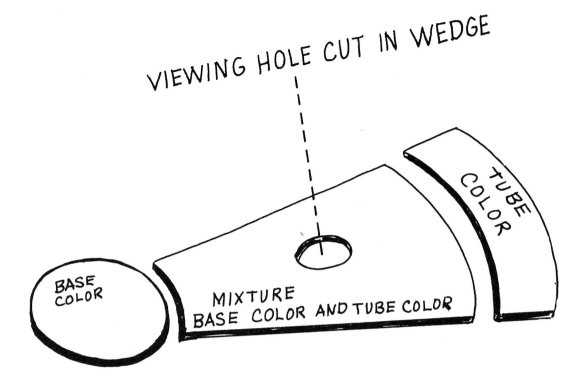

The colors between the center and the outside colors should represent mixtures of the inner and outer colors. Thus, you can use the color detector to find what colors are mixed to match a brown by using the detector disk that has a brown center. For shades of blue, use the one with the blue center. Always use the center color as your basic color. When you have selected the detector with the right color center, place it over the color to be matched and rotate the viewing holes until you have the closest match. The color to be matched may be lighter or darker, but it will give you an indication of which two colors to mix. If the color you wish to match is a light color, you may have to make a detector using whites added to the center colors. Experimentation will get you there. And experimenting with the detector avoids the potential catastrophe of mixing colors for, or on, your decoy. The detector can be placed over a photograph, painting, or study skin and will assist you in determining what paints to mix to get the desired color.

Mixing the Colors

When mixing colors, there is an imbalance in the mixing ratio. In other words, using equal parts, or a 50/50 mix, does not guarantee you will get the color that is midway between the two you started with. To magnify the problem, yellow does not have the pigment, or amount of color, that the red and blues may have. Yellow is the toughest of colors to apply over another without the original color showing through, because it is translucent, one that you can partially see through. It takes more coats of yellow to cover another color completely than it does red or blue, especially if a darker color is underneath.

Color Charts

Since you cannot usually buy exactly what you need, perhaps the time is right to make your own color chart. Knowing how to do something is only part of the answer; actually doing it—step by step—will etch it into your mind. It will also give you more self-confidence when you need to match a color.

The first step is to divide the paint into parts to control the mixing process. The most accurate method of mixing is by weighing, but since most of us do not have the equipment necessary to do this, we'll try a simpler way. I measured and marked equal sections on my palette with an indelible pen (one that would not rub off the wax). In order to conserve paints, I put some small tips on the end of my paint tubes. Most art stores have these tips, intended for painting directly from the tube, but they will not fit all brands. With tips on the tubes, I was able to control a fairly even flow along the lines I had created.

 DARK COLOR

 LIGHT COLOR

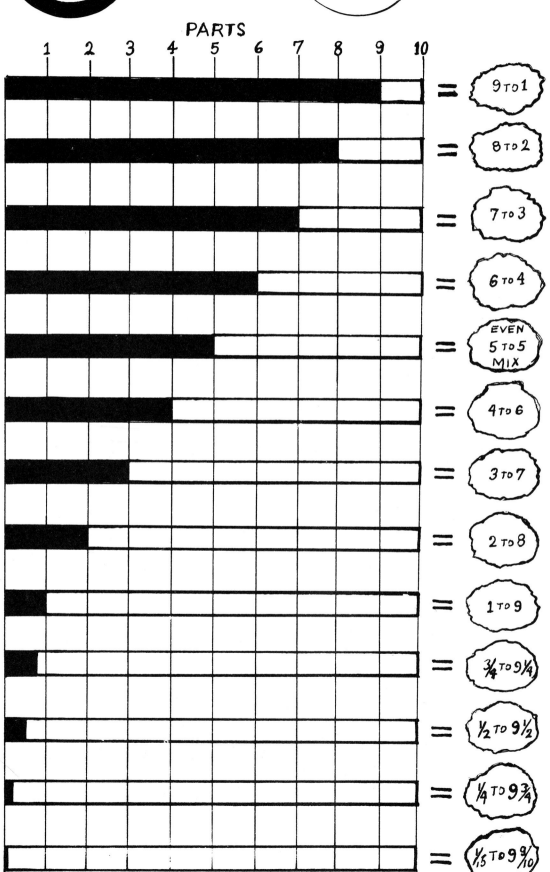

PARTS
1 2 3 4 5 6 7 8 9 10

= 9 TO 1

= 8 TO 2

= 7 TO 3

= 6 TO 4

= EVEN 5 TO 5 MIX

= 4 TO 6

= 3 TO 7

= 2 TO 8

= 1 TO 9

= 3/4 TO 9 1/4

= 1/2 TO 9 1/2

= 1/4 TO 9 3/4

= 1/15 TO 9 9/10

Color Chart

You can save the time of drawing these lines if you place wax paper over the chart on page 131 and measure the paint onto it. Remove the wax paper and use it as your palette to mix the paint. Before you start, though, make sure you have outlined a chart similar to those in the color section of this book. At least have something ready to put the paint on and keep a record of it.

The procedure is very simple. Mix nine parts of the dark color and one of the light color. Mix it thoroughly and paint a spot of it on your own color chart. Make sure the amounts or ratio of parts are written next to the painted spot. You can always refer back to it.

The next step is eight parts of the dark color and two of the light. Mix and paint another spot on your chart, always marking the ratio. Each step decreases the amount of dark color parts and increases the parts of lighter paint. You should always have a total of ten parts. I have shown the outcome of my experimental charts in the color section of this book.

I recommend that you start with the three primary colors for your charts. Use red as the dark and yellow as the light on the first chart. Then use blue as the dark color and yellow as the light color on the second; next, use blue as dark and red as light on the third.

If you have the time, try other dark and light tube colors. The experience will really pay off in the long run. Make sure that every mix is marked for future reference. Make a chart to show what happens when you add parts of the other primary color and, perhaps, black or white to the mixture of all three (using different ratios, naturally).

When you finish your own color charts you will have a permanent record to refer to whenever you feel uncertain about mixing colors as well as a better understanding of the process. If you mix colors and paint them everyday, it becomes easier and easier to do.

A problem with decoys is that when the carving is finished, you have to stop the flow of work you were just getting into. It is then time to paint—an entirely different type of work. When you finish painting the decoy, the flow of painting creativity will have to be interrupted until you can get another decoy carved.

With such inevitable problems it is very difficult to establish the kind of repetitious painting experience that ensures self-confidence. The mixing of paints and making of the charts is a sure way to recover more quickly each time. The word *recover* may throw you, but it is quite appropriate. If you do not carve regularly, you may have a tough time getting back into the swing again. It is almost like starting over, especially if some time has elapsed in between carvings. If this is a problem with carving, it is even more evident with painting. The interlude between painting sessions may be hours, weeks, or months, depending on the time you can devote to it. Actual use of the brush is not too difficult; rather the uncertainty of mixing colors presents the real problem. Your charts will bring everything back into focus quickly—no matter how long you are away from painting. The charts are worth every bit of time you can spend on them.

Painting Tips

We have already discussed the primary colors red, yellow, and blue, but I want you to remember them without having to look up the definition. All other colors come from red, yellow, and blue, although there are limitations depending upon which shades of each are used. The most vivid or brilliant colors that you can buy in tubes *cannot* be mixed from other tube colors. You may be able to approximate the color, but it will lack the brilliance. This doesn't mean that it shines; by *brilliant*, I mean it is bright with color. This factor keeps us from buying just the primary colors.

The Basic Mixes

Orange is made by mixing red and yellow.
Violet is made by mixing red and blue.
Green is made by mixing blue and yellow.
Brown is made by mixing red, yellow, and black (dark blue may be substituted for black in some shades).
Gray is made by mixing black and white (shaded with blue or brown).
Sky blues are made by mixing blue and white and adding yellow or red.
The natural colors of nature are mixtures of the three primary colors plus black or white. Flesh color, for instance, is a mixture of all the primary colors and white (in proper proportion).

Things I Learned the Hard Way

Dark colors eat light colors; a lighter color applied over a dark color will darken and diminish in color after the paint dries and cures. The color you paint on a dark background one night will not be as light a few nights later. There are advantages to this because it enables you to bring the color up to the desired lightness gradually by using several coats.

All colors applied over a white background will be more vivid and decorative but will lose the tones of depth created by texturing. If you use acrylics, use *lots of water*. It's cheap; use lots of it. Beginners are afraid to thin acrylics to achieve the proper flow of paint from the brush. Jump in and splash it around—water is the secret to using acrylics.

Blending can be done very effectively with acrylics if you dampen the surface to be painted before you start painting. Even though the surface to be painted may be well-sealed and several coats of acrylics applied, it will still react like a sponge and absorb some of the moisture. Retaining the wetness allows time for the paints to blend. Put the moisture there before you start, and the working time of acrylics will be extended.

Boldness should be practiced with acrylics. If you paint a room at home and don't like the color, you can always paint another color over it. The same goes for the decoy; do not be afraid that you will make a mistake. Mistakes can be corrected, so jump in and move that paint around. Remember: The bolder you get with acrylics, the better you get with acrylics.

A wetting agent, added to the water, will improve the flow of paint. There are commercial products available that will make water wetter.

Here are some tips on proper care of your paintbrushes. Alcohol can be used to remove dried acrylic paint in brushes. Soap and water are excellent for cleaning brushes before you put them away. Store brushes in an upright position with the bristles to the top. If the brush is left flat or lying down, it might get shoved against something and cause the bristles to take an unfortunate set.

Hardened acrylics in a brush can be removed by immersing only the bristles in hot water and detergent. Bring the water to a boil, turn the heat off, and add detergent. Do not put the metal part of the brush into hot water; it may cause damage to the agent holding the bristles together. Clean the loosened paint from the center of the brush with the aid of a round toothpick.

You can mix any three tube colors together, but the addition of a fourth will cause the mixture to turn muddy.

A single color is rarely used straight from the tube. To produce nature's colors, it should be tinted with another color.

Acrylics thinned too much will not adhere to a slick surface. Thick acrylics have the best adhesion for the first coat.

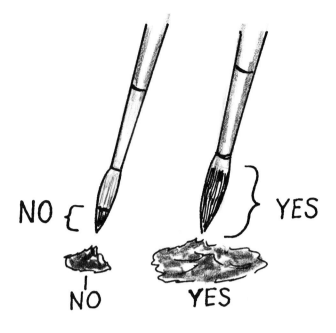

Don't skimp on paint—on the palette or in the brush. The larger brush will also hold more paint and yet the tip will remain the same approximate size.

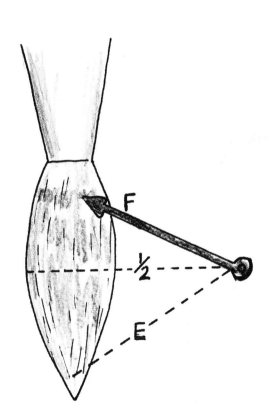

The full tank load. If you want to go on a trip, you start with a full tank. The same goes for painting; you'll only paint as long as the brush is filled.

The barrel of the brush is labeled so for good reason: It holds paint for you to use. The larger the barrel, the more paint it holds.

When using acrylics, use plenty of water. It does not have to be measured by the drop.

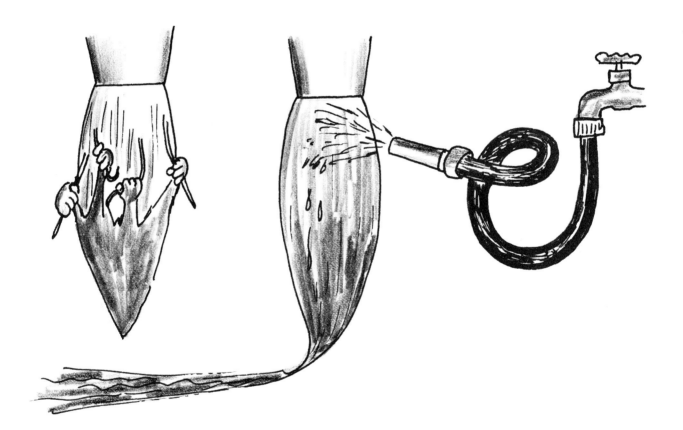

Thick paint will hold on to the brush and will not flow. Thinning it will not only load the brush better but will let if flow more evenly.

I use a lot of film canisters for various jobs. With the open end dipped in water and then set over a pile of acrylic on my palette, it will seal and keep the paint moist for a day or so. Paint mixed and placed in these containers will not dry out for extended periods. I also put thinners into them to clean brushes—less waste and mess.

My fancy brush holders. (Yes, I ate the Pringles first.)

The New Trend: Realistic Sculptures

The latest trend in the evolution of the decoy is realistic sculptures. It all started with the original hunting decoy of past generations and progressed step by step to full-bodied ducks with extended wings and tails, open mouths, and habitat backgrounds. From the initial blocks of wood to the assembly of many shaved or thin pieces, the decoy movement keeps advancing.

What is the next stage of the movement? How far can it go? Some would say it can't get any better; they've gone as far as the real things now! I say, "Hogwash!" Although most people are amazed at the likeness of the carvings to the real thing, we've a long way to go yet. Few people have observed live ducks or birds in the attitudes in which they are carved, at the same distance from which they will be viewed and handled. Being able to observe the details of a live bird at rest from two feet is a lot different from studying it through binoculars or a telephoto picture taken at 30 feet. It's just a matter of new perspectives, education, and time—the art will progress much further yet. *It will occur one step at a time.*

Mallard hen

Pintail hen

All sculptures are wood with the exception of the glass eyes and nails used in the legs. All sculptures were made by the author.

Pair of Green-winged Teals

Pair of Woodcocks. Although these are not ducks, they exemplify the impact the decoy movement has had in spreading to all birds.

Helpful Hints

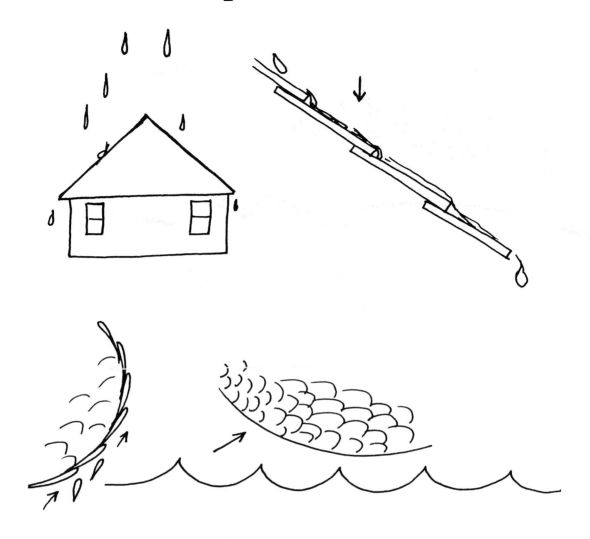

The shingling or overlap of feathers: Just as a house roof has to shed water from above, ducks have to be protected from the water as they splashdown or swim. The overlap is from front to rear and bottom to top (except for head, tertials, wing and tail).

Sidepocket—houses the wing underneath.

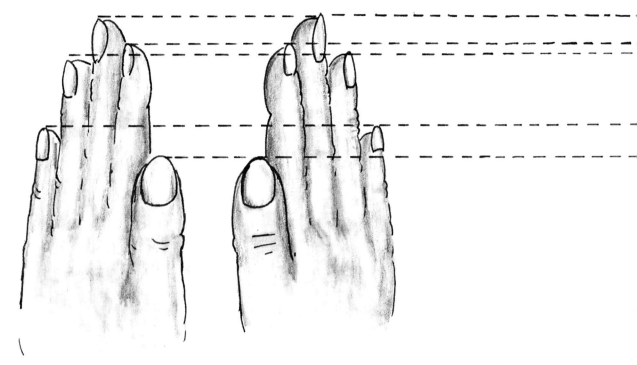

Easy reminder of the lengths of the tertials and their order of stacking.

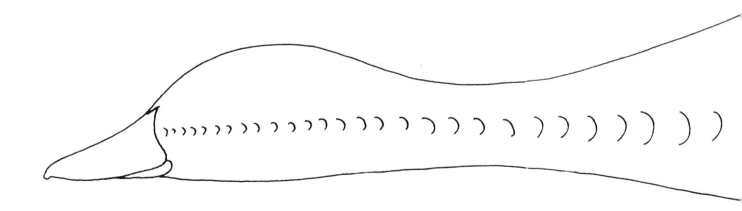

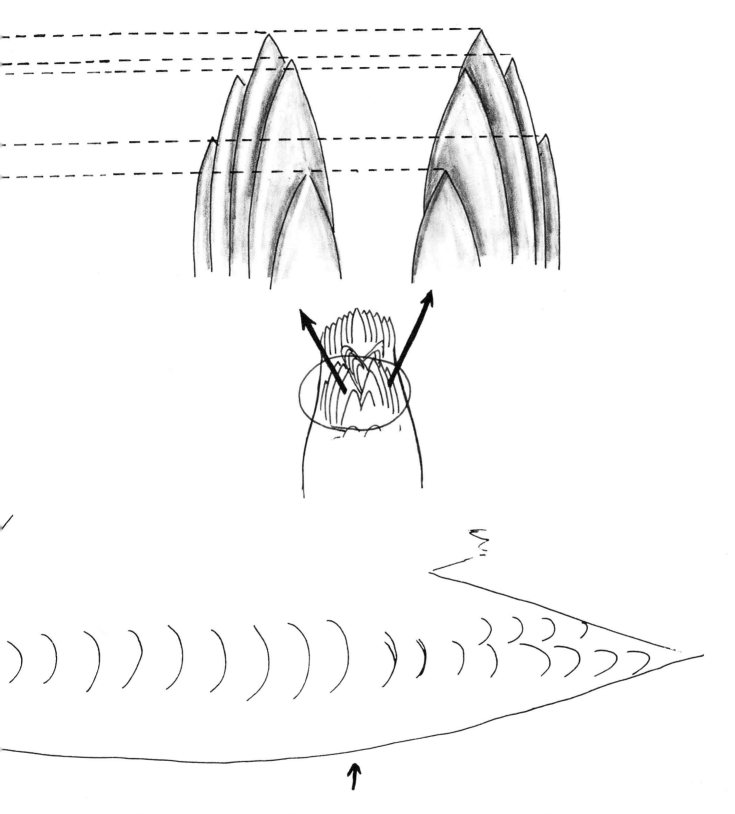

Duck feathers get progressively larger from front to rear, to the end of the sidepocket. At that point they diminish in size to the end of the body (not greatly, however).

The jowl and shoulder coverts are transitional sets of feathers—the hinge points of direction for feathers.

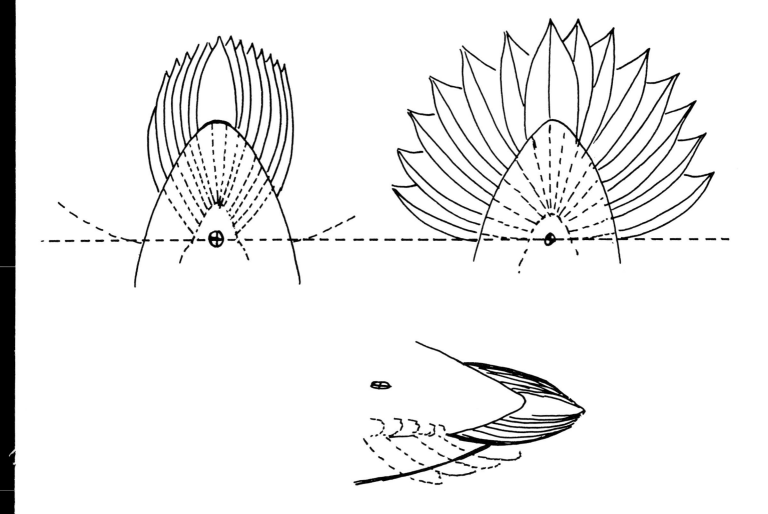

Center or swivel point for the tail: Note how the tail knifes out through feathers on the side and emerges from the body at various points depending on the motion of the duck.

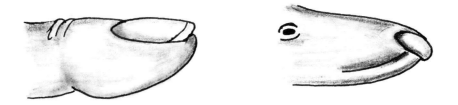

Note the similarity of the nail of the bill with your own fingernail.

Nature creates with gentle arcs and curves, such as those on sand dunes. Feathers, also created by nature, resemble these rolling features.

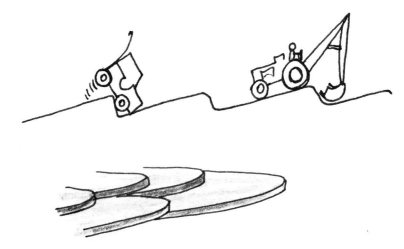

Humans create the sharp breaks and indentations with uniformity in mind. Feathers created as plates stacked as shown represent what human beings would like feathers to be.

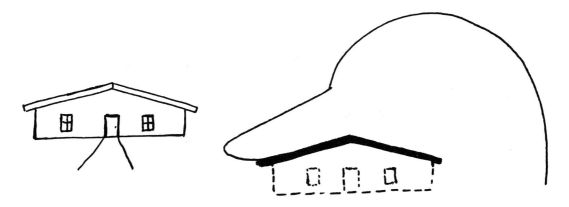

The proper perspective of bill to throat can be compared to the low pitch roof of a building.

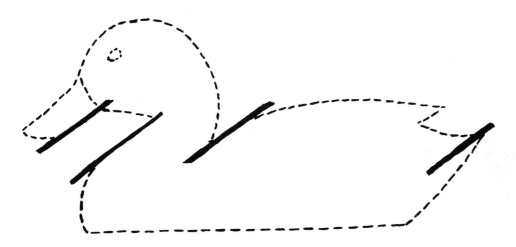

Four parallel lines describe bill, breast, shoulder, and tail of a duck at ease.

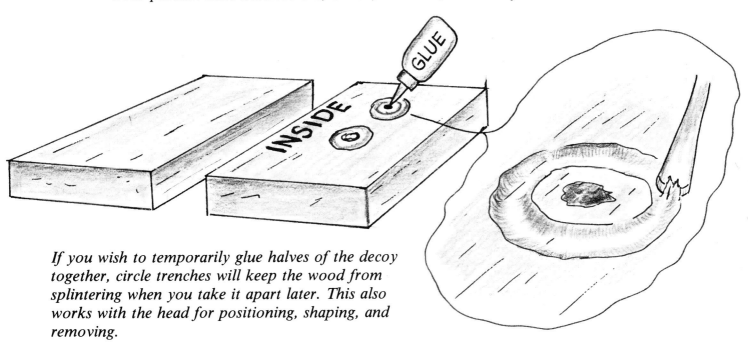

If you wish to temporarily glue halves of the decoy together, circle trenches will keep the wood from splintering when you take it apart later. This also works with the head for positioning, shaping, and removing.

Nail the blocks together if you do not have clamps. Angle the nails and do not pound them in all the way so they may be removed before sawing. Nails that are designed for removal can be purchased at most hardware or art supply stores.

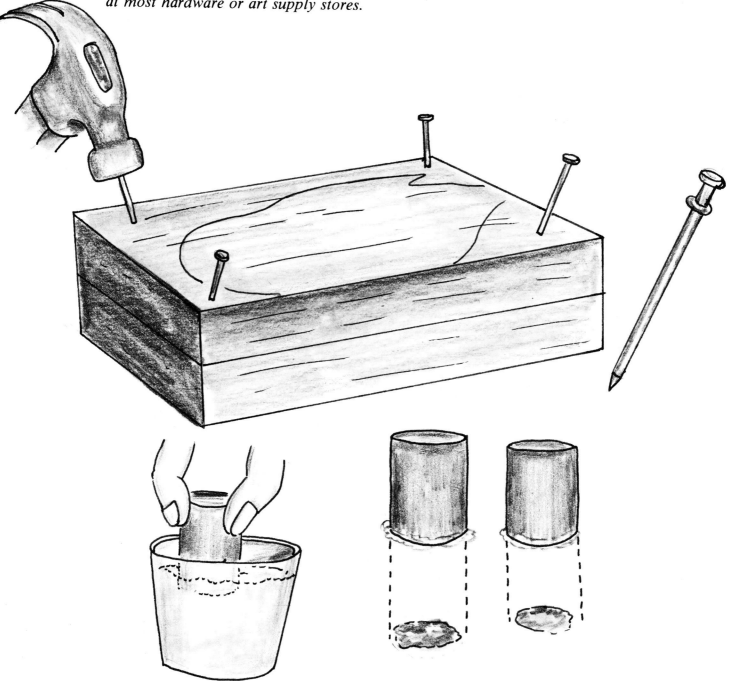

Film canisters, dipped in water and placed over wet acrylic, will preserve the paint overnight for you.

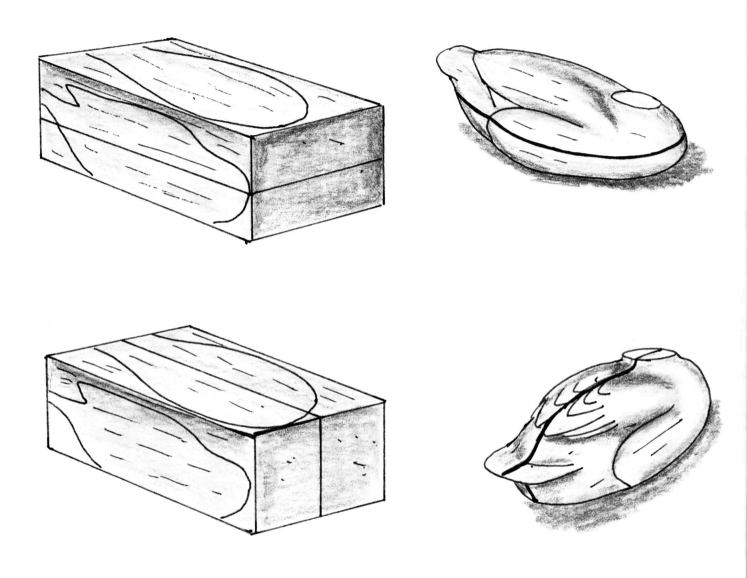

Blocks glued together for a decoy. One type will cause a seam that completely encircles the decoy and may create problems. The other will have a seam down the centerline of the body and will be easier to work into the feather detail. Also, it puts the seam through the bottom which won't usually be noticed.

The boldness and pattern of vermiculation differ on each species of duck. Beginning at the top the species shown are: Mallard, Wood Duck, Wigeon, and Gadwall.

Dry-brushing: A good stiff brush is best for dry-brushing or blending acrylics. Dip the dry brush into acrylic (no water added), wipe on a paper towel, and clean the rest of the brush on the area to blend. Repeat and build the color if necessary.

Glossary

Acrylics water-soluble, plastic-based paint.
Alkyds oil-based paint.
Automotive body filler plastic compound used for filling dents.
Axioms basic principles for carving anatomy.
Bandsaw power saw with continuous band blade.
Block wood to shape for decoy.
Blocks nickname for wood hunting decoys.
Bristles fibers of the brush used to hold paint.
Centerline a line establishing the exact center.
Color charts swatches or spots of paint mixes used for reference.
Color detector circular colored disks used to match colors.
Color wheel painting aid for mixing colors.
Coping saw a fine blade handsaw.
Crown top and forehead of the head.
Decoy simulated shape used for luring.
Diving ducks species that dive for food; they also run across water to take off.
Drake male duck.
Drawknife a two-handled cutting blade drawn to cut.
Eye trough the recessed area at front and rear of eye.
Fixture a jig or clamping device.
Flaws imperfections or errors.
Gesso a white paint (acrylic) used as a primer.
Grain texture of the wood running the length of the tree or board.

Grit   term for the roughness of sandpaper.

Guide   an aid to establish lines or areas.

Hen   female duck.

Iridescence   metallic appearing colors of certain feathers.

Jowl   jutting part of the jaw on the head.

Kiln-dried   treatment of wood to reduce moisture content.

Lobe   top points of bill where it meets the head.

Mask   aid used to view small areas at a time.

Miniature   small decoy.

Mount   a duck skin mounted by a taxidermist.

Neck ring   a narrow colored band of feathers around throat.

Oils   paints with oil base.

Old-timers   decoy carvers of the past.

Painting comb   a device used to create wavy lines in paint.

Pattern   a guide for shape.

Pigment   powdered color mixed into liquid to create paint.

Primaries   major feathers of the wings.

Puddle ducks   species that feed on the surface of a body of water; they spring from the water to take off.

Rasp   a rough file.

Razor knife   a small knife with disposable blades.

Realistic sculpture   carving of wood to simulate actual features.

Sidepocket   side of the duck covering the wing.

Skins   feathered skins taken from ducks.

Tertials   large feathers covering the inner rear above wings when folded.

Tube colors   tubes of paint purchased from art stores.

Vermiculation   wormlike, wavy lines on feathers.

Waterline   line established by level of water displaced by a floating duck.

Index

155